The Best of the Barrelman
(1938 — 1940)
Joseph R. Smallwood as the Barrelman

Edited by
William Connors

BOOKS BY WILLIAM CONNORS
The Street Cars of Old St. John's
Winds of History

The Best of the Barrelman
(1938 — 1940)
Joseph R. Smallwood as the Barrelman

Edited by
William Connors

Creative Publishers
St. John's, Newfoundland
1998

The publisher acknowledges the support of the Department of Tourism, Culture and Recreation, Government of Newfoundland and Labrador, towards the publication of this book.

We acknowledge the financial support of the Department for Canadian Heritage for our publishing program.

Cover: David Peckford, (from the original masthead drawing by Max Chambers, who was employed at the Newfoundland Airport, now known as Gander).

∝ Printed on acid-free paper

Published by
CREATIVE BOOK PUBLISHING
a division of 10366 Newfoundland Limited
a Robinson-Blackmore Printing & Publishing associated company
P.O. Box 8660, St. John's, Newfoundland A1B 3T7
Printed in Canada by:
ROBINSON-BLACKMORE PRINTING & PUBLISHING

Canadian Cataloguing in Publication Data

Smallwood, Joseph R., 1900-1991.

    The best of the Barrelman (1938-1940)

    Items originally broadcast on the Newfoundland radio program The Barrelman, and later published as a monthly newspaper.

    ISBN 1-895387-99-X

1. Newfoundland — Anecdotes.   2. Newfoundland —History.
3. Newfoundland — Miscellanea.   I. Connors, William, 1925-
II. Title.   III. Title: Barrelman.

FC2161.8.S63   1998   971.8'03   C98-950264-2
F1122.6.S63   1998

I wish to thank Frank O'Leary for permission to publish items from *The Barrelman*. All royalties from the sale of this publication will be directed to the Newfoundland Collection, Provincial Reference and Resource Library and to the Provincial Archives of Newfoundland and Labrador.

Acknowledgements

I am grateful to the following people who enabled me to compile this publication: Wayne Sturge, Still and Moving Images, Provincial Archives of Newfoundland and Labrador (PANL); Cyril F. Marshall, Alexandria, Ontario, for permission to use four photographs from the Holloway collection; the Staff of the Newfoundland Collection, Provincial Reference and Resource Library; Gail Weir, Centre for Newfoundland Studies, Memorial University of Newfoundland; and Margo Connors and Kathleen Connors.

In addition to *The Barrelman* newspaper, reference materials for the Introduction and the Biographical Note include: The St. John's *Daily News*; *Encyclopedia of Newfoundland and Labrador*; *The Smallwood Era*, F. Rowe; and *Media Sense: The Folklore-Popular Culture Continuum*, P. Narvaez and Martin Laba (eds.).

CONTENTS

Introduction

There are those of us who still remember evenings in the years between 1937 and 1943 when we would wait for the sound of a ship's bell — a family sipping tea around the kitchen table, a gathering in the parlour, or a crowding of neighbours in an outport kitchen. Homework was briefly put aside. The rattling and sloshing of dishes ceased. Small children were hushed and shooed outside to play or at the very least stilled. At the clang of a bell struck six times, laughter, chatter, and debate would fall silent. For fifteen minutes, at 6:45 Monday to Saturday, Newfoundlanders listened to The Barrelman — a show "dedicated to making Newfoundland better known to Newfoundlanders".

The Barrelman radio program was the inspiration of its creator and host, the Barrelman himself, Joseph R. Smallwood, later the first Premier of Newfoundland. In fifteen minutes, six nights a week, eleven months a year for six years, he displayed his own pride and love of Newfoundland and worked to make Newfoundlanders share in this pride. He informed us and reminded us about: our magnificent and diverse geography; the successes, and enduring potential of our economy; the chronicle of the great accomplishments individual and collective in our history; and our ability to imagine, entertain and teach through story in the tall tales of our folklore.

The Barrelman was sponsored by St. John's merchant, F.M. O'Leary. A series of narrated items, the program opened and closed to the sound of a ship's bell struck six times. Smallwood later explained that this was the nearest that one could get a ship's bell to 6:45, the time when the show aired. Between each narrated item the bell sounded once. The sounding of the bell of a ship thematically linked the items to the show's nautical name.

The title "The Barrelman" illustrates Smallwood's view of himself as a leader, as one who sets the course and gives directions. The significance of the title is not readily apparent to everyone today. The barrelman would be the sailor who climbed to the top of the masthead on a ship, and from the vantage point of a securely placed barrel, would then shout directions to the ship's captain. He would see a greater distance than anyone else and thus, set the course. This was also Smallwood's pseudonym in his column "From the Masthead" which appeared in the St. John's *Daily News*. One can speculate that it is due to his success as The Barrelman that Smallwood later became captain of the ship of state, leading Newfoundland into Confederation with Canada and remaining Premier of the province for twenty-three years.

In compiling material for the program, Smallwood presented the findings of his own research, but he also called on listeners and readers to contribute to building the pride of fellow Newfoundlanders:

You see, I am trying to show the world that Newfoundlanders are a smart people. I am trying to show that they always succeed, every time that they get a decent chance. Help me to prove this, by sending me cases you know about yourself.

Newfoundlanders responded to the Barrelman's appeal. They told their stories to each other through the voice of the Barrelman and through these stories the show came to belong to Newfoundlanders. On the eve of Smallwood's final broadcast as the Barrelman, the St. John's *Daily News* reported that he had received over 60,000 letters.

Everyone could feel the opportunity to participate in the program was available to them. Even I as a young boy felt this opportunity. Douglas Eaton and I were exploring on Signal Hill where we discovered a cannon ball which we took to my back garden on Cathedral Street. The next day after school we hurried down Garrison Hill, retrieved the cannon ball and made our way across Duckworth Street to the F.M. O'Leary building near the War Memorial. There we met with the Barrelman himself, Joseph R. Smallwood, and we presented him with the cannon ball. That night from radio station VONF, located in the Newfoundland Hotel, he made us feel that we were heroes and he announced the cannon ball would be donated to the Newfoundland Museum.

And so he told stories of boys and girls, of men and women, of people who are part of our recorded history such as Captain Bob Bartlett, and of brave strong people who birthed the babies, rescued neighbours or strangers in storms and who now are largely forgotten. He told stories of Newfoundlanders who excelled abroad and those whose ingenuity enabled others to prosper.

In addition to telling stories, Smallwood stirred Newfoundlanders to charitable action in the annual Fish-a-Man appeal. This campaign asked each fisherman to donate a salt-dried cod to be sold to the highest bidder. The proceeds of the sale were used by the Newfoundland Patriotic Association to buy comforts for the Newfoundlanders serving in the armed forces in World War II. The fishermen and their families responded to Smallwood's appeal. The St. John's *Daily News* notes that over $50,000 was collected in the four years that Smallwood canvassed on air for the appeal.

The Barrelman was first aired on October 18, 1937 and its popularity soon grew. Yet it was not available to all Newfoundlanders. Many homes did not have radios; some communities had difficulty picking up radio stations from St. John's. In his zeal to reach as many Newfoundlanders as possible with his spirit and message of Newfoundland patriotism and pride, Smallwood began publication of *The Barrelman*, a monthly tabloid newspaper, in June, 1938. This paper published the best of the radio program so that every family in the country could read it. The initial run of the paper was 20,000 copies. A year later circulation increased to 25,000 copies distributed to 1300 settlements. Unfortunately, the only known copies of this paper available today date from June, 1938 to December, 1940. These newspapers and the original radio scripts were donated by Frank O'Leary, son of the sponsor of The Barrelman to the Centre for Newfoundland Studies, Memorial University. The original copies of *The Barrelman* newspaper are now a resource in the Newfoundland section of the Provincial Reference and Resource Library where I gathered the material for this book. *The Barrelman* did not contain photographs. I have selected the photographs contained in this book to complement *The Barrelman* entries.

Smallwood once said that in producing The Barrelman he aimed to stir, create and fan Newfoundland patriotism; that he tried "to destroy the horrible inferiority complex that our people had." He told his listeners and readers: "There are some people, you know, who don't think very much of us Newfoundlanders. Let us prove to them that Newfoundlanders have courage, brains, strength, great powers of endurance." Smallwood called on the Newfoundland people to take part in his mission:

Send me stories — true stories — showing how brave are the Newfoundlanders; how hardy they are; how strong they are; what hardships they endure.

He urged: "Let us show them that Newfoundlanders are witty and smart." In calling us to show ourselves to others, he showed us ourselves.

I hope that the items I have selected from the best of the extant *Barrelman* newspapers will bring back memories to those who once listened to The Barrelman and make history a little more accessible to those who did not. I hope also that we as Newfoundlanders and Labradorians will once again be stirred by Joseph Smallwood's vision of ourselves and remember that we continue to be brave, and strong and smart.

Joseph R. Smallwood (1900-1991)
Biographical Note

Although called "the little fellow from Gambo", Smallwood and his family moved to St. John's soon after his birth. He was educated at a number of city schools including Bishop Feild. In 1915, he left school to work as an apprentice at a city newspaper. Between 1918 and 1924 he worked for newspapers in St. John's, Halifax, Boston and New York. He then returned to Newfoundland as labour organizer and a socialist. Later, being pragmatic, Smallwood became a liberal. He married Miss Clara Oates in 1925.

In the first decades of his marriage Smallwood wrote *Coaker of Newfoundland* and *The New Newfoundland*; he established the *Humber Herald*, managed Sir Richard Squires' campaign of 1928 and helped organize the new fishermen's union in Bonavista. In 1936 he began the two-volume *The Book of Newfoundland* (now six volumes). The set contains articles on the history, institutions and topical events of Newfoundland and was intended to "restore the faith of Newfoundlanders in their country." Smallwood then began his column *From the Masthead* by the Barrelman for the St. John's *Daily News* and, in 1937, began his radio career as the same.

In 1939 Smallwood acted on a life-long interest in farming and established a farm on the outskirts of St. John's. He retired from The Barrelman to run a pig farm in Gander four years later. Michael Harrington then hosted The Barrelman until the show went off the air in 1956.

1946 brought the National Convention — an elected body to recommend the future form of government for Newfoundland. Smallwood was elected as a member for Bonavista Centre. "With his superb oratorical skills and matchless memory, Smallwood dominated the Convention," states Frederick Rowe, politician and historian, in his book *The Smallwood Era*. In the convention forum Smallwood advocated and worked for Confederation with Canada converting thousands of Newfoundlanders who listened to him by radio.

Joseph Smallwood became the first Premier of Newfoundland in 1949 and he remained Premier until 1972. In keeping with his positive vision of Newfoundland, one of Smallwood's first acts after becoming Premier was to raise the status of Memorial University College to a University. On retirement from politics, he continued writing and began another project *The Encyclopedia of Newfoundland and Labrador*. Smallwood suffered a stroke in 1984. Smallwood, the prodigious writer and great orator, could neither speak nor write. The encyclopedia project was in financial difficulties and was finished due to a group of interested and committed citizens. At the time of his death, in 1991, three volumes of the five volume set had been published.

Smallwood's political style, as well as his accomplishments and failures as a premier, will be analyzed and debated by historians. His love, vision and passion for Newfoundland and Labrador remain a legacy and inspiration for us all in his numerous writings and, most especially in the projects he initiated — *The Book of Newfoundland* and *The Encyclopedia of Newfoundland and Labrador*.

SEALS AND SEALERS

Their Lives Two Seals Save

March 1940

You're not going to read now the tragic story of the Greenland disaster in 1898—that terrible catastrophe that sent a chill of horror through the country—but only one of many incidents that happened in connection with it, as part of it.

It is told by Mr. Joseph Howell a native of Newtown, Bonavista Bay, now a resident of St. John's. He was on her at the time. He was one of the three watches of fifty men each that left the *Greenland* at dawn that Monday morning on the 21st of March to look for seals. Mr. Howell's watch tramped over the ice all that forenoon looking for seals, but finding none they turned about at dinner-time and started the return journey to the ship. The *Greenland* was then sixty or seventy miles northeast of the Funks—out in the open ocean—and the men were about twelve miles from the ship. When they got to within seven miles of her they came to a great open pond of water where the ice had separated, making it impossible for them just then to proceed any further. That was about four o'clock in the afternoon.

They had no sooner reached the edge of this open water than it began to snow. The snow began to fall more and more thickly, and then the wind began to rise. It increased in volume every few minutes, and the temperature dropped very rapidly. Before they knew it they were in the midst of one of the most terrible howling blizzards ever experienced at the icefields. And then, when it seemed as though human nature just couldn't stand it, the storm got even worse, with the snow swirling fiercely into their faces, until they looked like snow-men, the wind tearing down in devastating blasts upon them, and the frost growing more deadly intense.

The fifty men got separated, only fifteen being in the group that included Mr. Howell. These fifteen men started in to build an ice-wall to form some little shelter. But the chunks and pieces of ice would be whipped away in the wind, until they hit on the idea of using wet, sticky snow as a sort of cement to bind them. Eventually they got a wall three feet high and six feet long, down behind which they clustered together and crouched away from the fullest force of the storm. That was seven o'clock that night, three hours having been occupied in building it. At times the howling tornado of wind threatened to whip the ice-wall away, but by straining with all their might against it the fifteen men managed to keep it in place.

And then occurred the remarkable event which undoubtedly saved their lives that night of terror. Two young seals, apparently blinded by the storm, came toward them and in a flash were captured by the men. They were just going to kill the two seals when somebody spoke up and protested, saying that the seals would be far more useful to them alive than dead. Quickly he explained what he meant, and they agreed with his idea and started at once to carry it out. This was to use the hot-blooded young seals as living stoves. Taking turns, the men sprawled their

1

bodies over the seal, hugging the warm young seals close to them, and absorbing the heat from it. Perhaps five minutes, perhaps ten or fifteen, each man would have for his turn, by which time new heat coursed through his own veins.

All night long they kept this up, and we get the amazing spectacle of fifteen human lives being saved by two seals. Their lives were saved, yes—but without food, and exposed still to the terrible storm that howled for five hundred miles around them on the open ocean, they were a pitiable little group of men when dawn broke that Tuesday morning. They must have more heat—they must. Someone thought of their gaffs—why not use them to make a fire? But the gaffs were thirty or forty feet away from them. But by linking arms they made a human chain that reached and handed back the gaffs, one by one. Then a desperate struggle to keep a match lit long enough to start a fire—this took two hours.

At two o'clock that afternoon they killed the two seals and ate the edible parts, using the oily fat to keep the fire going behind the wall of ice. A four o'clock that afternoon the storm died suddenly away, and they could see their ship seven miles away. At seven o'clock that night they climbed wearily up over the side to safety at last—safety and warmth and food—to find, alas, that forty-eight of their comrades never again would greet them on earth—forty-eight gallant New-foundlanders who joined the great throng of victims of the storm king during the past three hundred years.

Copying

Miraculous Escape

May 1939

Of all the miraculous escapes from death that have occurred around the coast of Newfoundland—and of course there have been a great many thousands—one of the most amazing of all is the one experienced by the late William Woodfine, of Torbay

It happened about sixty years ago, the year the seals came in upon the coast in thousands—lots of people living today will remember the spring I mean. It happened on an Easter Sunday morning.

A large number of men from Torbay, as from other settlements along the St. John's shore, went out on the ice after the seals, William Woodfine being one of them. They weren't out very long before a thick fog descended and blanketed the land, so there was an immediate rush to get back to shore. Most of them got back, but some weren't so fortunate. Captain Jackman, passing along the shore on his way to his second trip that spring, picked up one group of men and put back to St. John's to land them.

William Woodfine was eventually the only one to be unaccounted for, and as a matter of fact he was drifted to the southward until he was directly off Cape Spear. He had a tow of four seals, and these he refused to abandon. In fact, it was while hauling these over the ice off Cape Spear that he plunged on two different occasions through the ice into the water.

And a lucky thing indeed it was for him that he didn't abandon his pelts, for on the second occasion he fell through the ice into the water he discovered, when he came up to the surface, that there wasn't a sizable piece of ice—not a piece big enough to keep him afloat—anywhere within his reach, and he couldn't swim a stroke. But right beside him was the tow of four pelts.

He climbed up on the pelts, which were just able to keep him afloat, and on this strangest of all rafts that I ever heard of he continued to drift to the southward until, just off Petty Harbour, he floated beside a pan of ice large enough to hold him up. He transferred himself to this, and hauled the pelts on with him. The pan of ice drifted into Petty Harbour, where he landed at eight o'clock on Tuesday morning, after spending all Sunday night, and Monday and Monday night alone on the raft of pelts and the small pan of ice.

Such was the characteristic Newfoundland stamina of the man that after a hot meal gladly given him by the Petty Harbour people, he refused all invitations to remain for a while, but started off on his twenty mile walk back to his home in Torbay—every inch a Newfoundland hero.

Walked Home From The Icefields

March 1939

Mr. Arch Webber of the city sends a most interesting account of an adventure which he, in company with a number of other men, had at the Icefields in the Spring of 1902. He was a member of the sealing steamer Kite, commanded that Spring by Captain Dan Greene. The Kite left St. John's one day ahead of the other ships. They had just reached Cape St. Francis when some trouble developed in their engine, and had to put back to port. The tug Ingraham wanted $500 for towing her in, but the Captain demurred at this and ordered the ship's sails hoisted. Bowring's own tug gave a pluck into the harbour. The famous Sealers' Strike was in progress when they got in, and they had to remain here till the strike was finally settled.

On the 12th of March they sailed again. They struck a few seals off Cape Fogo, but the wind sprang up from the North-East and they steamed across to White Bay, where they succeeded in getting jammed in the ice for a whole month.

Their food began to run very low, and finally the crew were put on rations—the principal item of food consisting of one pound of hard bread every twenty-four hours. Dissatisfaction began to develop amongst the men, who had visions of having to spend another month or more in the ice, and thereby losing their Summer's work and wages.

After some talk to this effect some twenty-two of the men decided to leave the ship and return home. Now, that sounds very easy, but remember that the *Kite* was jammed solidly in the ice just inside of Partridge Point, and most of them were hundreds of miles from their homes. It took a lot of nerve to make the attempt, but make it these twenty-two men did. At five o'clock on a Monday morning they climbed over the steamer's side, and started off over the ice.

The ice began to loosen up after they'd been travelling a short while, and their own means of progress was to use pans of ice as ferries to get across the ponds of open water. For two whole days and nights they travelled across the ice, and then reached the bottom of White Bay. Here their food had given out, and they had nothing whatever to eat but some dry coffee.

They saw a house ashore, and at this house, they managed to get a mug-up and a scant meal—the best its owner, with proverbial Newfoundland hospitality, could give them. As they left he gave them also some bread and pickled trout to take with them, and with no other food in their possession they started on their long hike across the frozen countryside to the main line of railway.

On their first stop at nightfall they put the trout in some fresh water to be ready for the morning, but imagine their disgust and disappointment, next morning to find the trout turning white when they began to roast them! They were white with salt, and quite unpalatable—they just couldn't eat them.

For five days they walked, and rested for a few hours each night—and all this time their only food was marshberries they managed to pick as they travelled along. At eleven o'clock on Friday morning they arrived at Howley, after a walk of five days.

On the way along the party had become divided into two—five of the men pushed on faster than the others, and these five had actually arrived in St. John's before the others arrived at Howley Station. They telegraphed to Sir Robert Bond at Whitbourne for passes, and the Prime Minister was instrumental in getting the passes for them.

They arrived in the city at noon on Saturday, not one bit the worse for their experience. Besides the writer of this account, Arch Webber, Mr. Harry Holwell, of the Furness Withy Company, and a Mr. Carrigan of Logy Bay, were among the party of five who arrived here first.

Men hauling seal pelts to their ship

Lost Nine Days on Ice

July 1938

I love to hear, and repeat, stories illustrating the great courage and powers of endurance of the Newfoundlander. I doubt very much if there's another race in the world with the powers of endurance equal to that of the Newfoundlander. Here's one of these stories received the other day from a correspondent.

It's about a man named Jonathan Gosse, a native of Spaniard's Bay, where he lived 'til he was 40 years of age. Then he settled in Indian Islands, Fogo District.

The second year he was in Indian Islands the seals came well in toward the land, and he was one of the men who struck out from the shore seal hunting. While he was out on the ice the wind shifted suddenly, the ice broke away from the land, and there was no possible means of his getting back. He drifted with the ice, and as he got near the Wadham Islands made several attempts to land there. He didn't succeed, and all he got for his trouble was a ducking in the icy water.

The ice continued to drift until he found himself, three days later, off Cape Freels. He could see the people on the land, and made frantic efforts to attract their attention. He could see them—but they couldn't see him—and the ice continued its southerly drift. Gosse kept alive by eating scraps of seal meat and snow.

On the ninth day of his drift he was some miles off the bill of Cape Bonavista, and he was about giving up hope. Then Capt. Charlie Dawe, of Bay Roberts, returning from the icefields in the *Terra Nova*, sighted the man on the ice, and had him brought aboard.

Although Jonathan Gosse never got over the effects of his terrible experience, he lived for fifteen years afterwards and died at Dildo, where he has a brother living today.

* * *

Martin Jennings of Codroy Valley

October 1940

Here's Mrs. Patrick Dolan again and she tells us of that colourful character from out the pages of Codroy Valley's past, Martin Jennings.

"I have told you," says Mrs. Dolan,'so many stories about Martin Jennings that you must wonder if he was man or myth. Nevertheless I give it to you as truth."

"John McKean was a young man who had never been to the icefields before. As his vessel hove-to beside a pan of seals he leaped over her side. He was only a few yards from the vessel when his feet slipped from under him and he sprawled on his back in the path of an oncoming dog hood. Pandemonium broke out on board, with men shouting and bawling.

"Silence! roared the voice of one accustomed to authority, and save for the grinding of the ship's side against the ice, silence reigned. The seal with fangs

6

bared was already upon John McKean when Martin Jennings raised his musket to his shoulder.

"Don't shoot! you'll kill the man! roared the captain.

"'No more for me to kill him than the seal," retorted Martin Jennings, as he pressed the trigger. The seal fell dead. It was shot through the eye, and before it was removed from the unconscious but uninjured man, someone in the crowd pointed out to the rest that the mouth of the seal was a scant three fingers from John McKean's throat."

* * *

Three Times They Went

August 1939

Of course you know that it used to be pretty common for the sealing ships in the old days to make a second trip to the icefields every spring, but I bet you weren't so familiar with the fact that they sometimes used to make even a third trip.

Mr. A.E. Worrall of the city has been good enough to send me a list, compiled from Chafe's Sealing Book, of the steamers that made third trips.

In 1869 the steamship *Hawk*, under Captain William Jackman, made a third trip. So did the *Nimrod*, under Capt. Edward White, and that another steamer that made a third trip in 1878 was the *Walrus*, under Captain Mark Delaney. The *Walrus* made a third trip in 1880, under Captain Job Barbour. This was the last time a third trip was made in one spring—the *Walrus* in 1880. She was not as able as the other ships to force her way through the ice, and this was the cause of her being so successful that year. She struck her first load off Torbay, her second off Pouch Cove, her third off St. John's. The seals were so plentiful that year off the city that hundreds of men walked off and brought them in by thousands.

* * *

The Clever Arthur Jackman

July 1938

It isn't so many years ago since the sealing fleet in St. John's could be divided roughly into two classes—those ships that were sailed by Newfoundland captains, and those sailed by skippers from Dundee.

Needless to say, there was the keenest possible rivalry between the Newfoundland captains and the Dundee men. Those old Dundee skippers were no slouches, and the struggle to be first to load and back in St. John's was very keen every spring.

One of the Dundee men was a Captain Fairweather, an old Scotsman who died only a few years ago in Scotland at the age of 90 or more. One spring Captain Fairweather made up his mind that he was going to be the first to bring his ship home loaded to St. John's.

The greatest of the native captains at the time was the famous Captain Arthur Jackman. From the moment they started off through the narrows the majority of the captains tried to keep Captain Arthur Jackman in sight. With equal determination Captain Arthur tried to shake them off, all but one—Captain Fairweather. the Scotsman kept doggedly in his wake. This was the situation when Capt. Jackman spied the seals ahead late in the afternoon. He gave orders to stop the ship and burn down for the night.

Up came Capt. Fairweather a quarter of a mile behind and sent word to enquire what the trouble was.

Capt. Arthur replied, "Dirty weather—no use going any further tonight—I'll wait til morning."

"I'll do the same," said the Scotsman. "What time will you start in the morning?"

"I'll tell you what," said Capt. Jackman, "I'll hang a red lantern on the stern so you can see me all night." And so they arranged it.

I don't suppose there's much need to tell you the rest. When daybreak came you can imagine the Scotsman's disgust to find Jackman gone out of sight, and the red lantern that he had seen all night still standing on the end of a pole that Capt. Arthur had stood up in the ice.

Capt. Arthur arrived home first with a full load, and Capt. Fairweather got back clean.

FAMOUS NEWFOUNDLANDERS
The Great Captain Bob

June 1940

Is there in all Newfoundland today a man, woman or child who hasn't heard of Captain Bob Bartlett? Without a doubt he's the most world-famous Newfoundlander living anywhere in the world today—not only that: he's one of the most internationally famous explorers and adventurers of any nationality in the world today.

All the world knows of his many expeditions into the frozen Arctic—of his historic voyage to the North Pole with Commander Peary—of his marvellous exploit in connection with the loss of the *Karluk*—and of his numerous voyages to Greenland and even farther north in his famous schooner, the *Morrissey*. Our fellow countryman's name is a veritable household word in the United States and Canada.

Perhaps of many thrilling adventures Captain Bob has had in his wonderful career as an explorer was the time his *Karluk* got crushed in the ice and sank to the bottom in Arctic water.

She was the flag-ship of Stephansson's expedition in 1913—1916. On the eleventh of January, 1914, the *Karluk* sank to the bottom, and Captain Bob proceeded to get all his men ashore many miles distant over the ice to Wrangell Island, where they made camp. That was on March the 12th.

On March the 18th, Captain Bob proceeded to put into execution an almost unbelievably daring plan he had thought up to bring relief to the shipwrecked men. With a pack of seven dogs hauling a sledge, and accompanied by one man, an Eskimo, Bob started out to walk across the ice a distance of two-hundred-miles to the coast of Siberia. Starting off in a howling gale of drifting snow on March the 18th, he sighted land on the thirtieth of that same month, and reached it three days later, having gone through experiences and exposure and hardship that not another two white men in the whole world could have endured.

But at the part of Siberia where they landed there were no livyers, and he had to strike down the coast along the shores of the Bering Straight, until he finally came to some tribes of Eskimos from whom he tried to buy or borrow some dogs to take the place of his own, which were worn out from the long hike over the rough ice.

Thirty-seven days after starting out from Wrangell Island Captain Bob finally arrived at Nome, having walked the staggering total of seven hundred miles. Nearly all the hair had been worn off his head by the hood he wore, and he had a beard that came down to his chest—in fact, when he washed and shaved he scarcely knew himself when he looked in the glass!

Then his legs began to swell out of shape, his eyes were bloodshot, and he was so stiff and sore that he could hardly move a hand. During those thirty-seven days he had lost forty pounds of his weight. It was a super-human effort—one of the mightiest personal achievements history has ever recorded. On arrival at Nome he telegraphed the Canadian Government the news, and they sent the steamship *Bear*—the old Newfoundland sealing ship—to the rescue, and in September they arrived at Wrangell Island just in the nick of time to save those who had survived since March.

Capt. Bob Bartlett aboard the *Effie Morrissey*.

Sir Ambrose Shea Great Newfoundlander

July 1940

In the year 1886 Sir Ambrose Shea was nominated by the Crown to be Governor of Newfoundland—the only case on record when a Newfoundlander ever came within a mile of being Governor of his native country.

Sir Ambrose was then sixty-nine years of age, but he never actually occupied the office of Governor, and was in the following year, 1887, appointed Governor of another British Colony, The Bahama Islands, the second most northerly of the West Indian group of islands. He served as Governor of the Bahamas for eight years and in that period he made an impression on the people that won't be forgotten down there for another hundred years.

When first he went to the Bahamas he wasn't there very long before he noticed that the people all seemed anxious to get rid of a certain coarse cactus plant, known as the sisal, which introduced its noxious presence everywhere to the injury of less hardy but more useful plants. People were willing to pay good money to have it killed and uprooted—this had been going on for years, and by the time Sir Ambrose Shea got there, the cactus plant, though not so prevalent as in former years, was still a nuisance.

Sir Ambrose became interested in the people and in their problems and he began to study this problem of the sisal plant. The upshot of his study was that he discovered that the cactus could be made into the most perfect and valuable hemp. He began to convert the people to the idea of growing it—actually cultivate it. And hard work it proved—on all sides he was met with unbelief and scepticism.

He persevered however and actually demonstrated that the plant, when properly treated, produced the finest hemp known. And then, thanks to the Newfoundlander's great perseverance, the idea suddenly took on, and there was a rush to get into the new industry.

Sir Ambrose Shea (1815-1905)

Within three years no less than $600,000 had been invested in it, and within

11

another few years the Bahamas were exporting hemp to the value of $15,000,000 a year. At the very lowest estimate the fibre amounted to half a ton per acre, and was worth from one to two hundred dollars per ton. At first wealthy individuals and companies tried to snap up all the Crown lands to monopolize them, but Sir Ambrose stepped in and arranged for every family head on the islands to become land-owners, whether they wished it or not.

The new sisal industry was the making of the Bahamas. Then Sir Ambrose introduced a new banking system into the islands. He succeeded in establishing submarine cable connection with the mainland of America, as well as modern steamship connections.

Altogether, without a single doubt, Sir Ambrose Shea was one of the greatest Newfoundlanders who ever lived.

* * *

He Invented The Codtrap

September 1938

Capt. George Whitely writes a most interesting reply to the question I put on the air the other night—Who was the first man to set a codtrap in Newfoundland? Captain Whiteley's father was, of course, the inventor of the codtrap.

Says Capt. Whiteley: "After using it for three years my father gave the model to Capt. J. Joy, who was agent for Job Brothers in the Straits. Capt. Joy showed it to Mr. Stephen Rendell, father of Mr. Rendell, who was manager of Job Brothers in St. John's. Mr. Rendell sent it to the Boston Net and Twine Company and had one made the same size. When this one arrived Mr. Rendell persuaded John Snow of Kitty Vitty, one of their biggest dealers, to try it.

"The first year it was in use it was called a failure, but Mr. Rendell asked Mr. Snow to try it again the second year. He did so, and trapped a big voyage. The manager and owner of the Boston Net and Twine Co. wrote Capt. Whiteley's father and advised him to take out patent rights. This the inventor of the codtrap failed to do until it was too late.

"Here is how the codtrap got its name: Capt. Joseph Barbour, the grandfather of Mr. Max Barbour, manager of the Anglo-American Telegraph Company, was the first Newfoundland skipper to sail west up through the Straits looking for fish. Out with his cod seine one day in the Straits, he came across the codtrap set in a cove near Bonne Esperance. He was so curious to know what it was that he went ashore to ask Mr. Whiteley what it was called. Mr. Whiteley was then the principal fur buyer on the coast. He was familiar with all kinds of traps to catch animals, so he said to Capt. Barbour: "I call it the trap to catch fish, and that's what it was ever afterwards called, "the codtrap."

One of Mr. Whiteley's best friends on the Labrador Coast was a man who was the agent in charge of the Hudson's Bay Company post at Mingan. They used to exchange books. When this Smith was ordered by his company to Cartwright, he came down the coast and spent a few days with Mr. Whiteley at Bonne Esperance. When the two men parted they never expected to meet again.

12

Forty years afterwards Mr. Whiteley was in London, and the first man he sought out was Donald Smith—but he wasn't Donald Smith anymore—he was the famous Lord Strathcona, or as the Queen used to call him, "His Labrador Lordship." Mr. Whiteley was invited by Lord Strathcona to a private dinner party. Amongst the guests were the Prince of Wales, afterwards King Edward the VII, and Sir Thomas Shaughnessey, the President of the C.P.R.

SHIPS AND SHIPWRECKS

Terrible Wreck of the *Harpooner*

October 1938

In one of my recent broadcasts, I listed the steamship Arctic, the steamship Anglo-Saxon, the Lady Sherbrooke, and the sealing steamer, Southern Cross, as being in that order, the four most disastrous wrecks ever to occur in Newfoundland. The Southern Cross was not, however, the fourth worst wreck in the history of Newfoundland—she was the fifth.

The fourth, in which 208 lives were lost, was the transport ship *Harpooner* in 1816. The loss of the *Harpooner* was not alone the fourth most disastrous in the country's history of wrecks and loss of life at sea, but it was in many ways the most heart-breakingly tragic of all.

The *Harpooner* as I have said, was a transport ship. In the month of November, 1816, the *Harpooner* sailed from Quebec bound to England with 385 passengers aboard, not counting the crew. These passengers consisted of whole families—men, women and children—the male passengers being exclusively soldiers of different regiments of the British forces in North America. The largest number of them were made up of officers and soldiers belonging to the Fourth Royal Veteran Battalion. There were also some detachments of the Royal Artillery, the Artillery Drivers, and of six other regiments. They were returning with their families to England on their first furlough in many years. Many of the soldiers were veterans of the American War, and some of them were still suffering from wounds received in that war.

They had moderate weather down the St. Lawrence River and across the Gulf, and in fact all the way along the Southwest Coast of Newfoundland. Fog had prevailed for the last three days before the wreck on Sunday night, November 10th, and they hadn't been able to take any observations. At nine o'clock that Sunday night, at St. Shotts near Cape Pine, the big ship struck her bottom lightly on a submerged rock. she heeled over, righted herself again, and proceeded a short distance farther, when she struck much more heavily on another rock, and began rapidly to fill. She was now encircled by shoals and rocks of all kinds.

The captain called all hands forward, brought the ship around by her head, allowing the stern to swing round with her stem toward the shore. Just then the wind increased, and continued to increase till it blew a gale. By the captain's orders the masts were cut away—but unfortunately the large boats were smashed to splinters when she first struck, and at eleven o'clock, to make it worse, the remaining boats were carried away by the seas which swept over her deck.

Before the last boat was gone however, a mate and four seamen launched one and succeeded in getting in to the base of a large rock which rose to a height of 100 feet out of the water some distance off from the shore. They got in to this rock—but couldn't get out to the ship again through the boiling seas.

In the meantime everything on board was a scene of ghastly terror and

14

confusion. Nobody could get below—the ship was filled with water—and, to make matters worse, she was lying on her beam ends, and all the passengers were crowded on that part of the deck which was out of the water, clinging to the rigging, and anything else they could grasp.

Then the ship caught fire, and the panic became worse. They succeeded, however, in putting out this fire. There was nothing to do but wait for the break of dawn. When dawn did break an attempt was made to throw a log-line to the seamen on the rock. They failed in this, and then someone remembered a dog they had aboard. Quickly they tied a light line around the dog, pointed to the rock, and urged him over the side. The dog swam to the rock, the line was taken by one of the seamen, and by this means a heavier rope was hauled in from the ship to the rock.

Instantly there was a mad scramble amongst the passengers to get ashore by means of this rope. Others jumped overboard in the hope of being able to swim to the rock—but were dashed to their death amongst the reefs and smaller rocks in the water. Counting the five seamen on the rock, the total number saved out of the 385 passengers aboard was only 177—208 lost their lives.

Suddenly there was a shout from those on the rock—"Go forward! Go forward!" Those on the stern part of the ship couldn't hear, or else didn't understand, and they were lost when the stern part of the ship suddenly collapsed and they were washed away in the wreckage. By twelve o'clock that day nothing was left of the ship but a few pieces of floating debris amid the jagged rocks.

A couple of military officers walked a distance of 17 or 18 miles across some open marshes till they reached the settlement of Trepassey. There they reported the terrible wreck, and the parish priest and people of the settlement hurriedly sent back to the scene of the disaster all the food they could get together. In the meantime, on the rock itself, you can imagine the day and night of terror and suffering of the survivors. Very few of the men, women and children had more than their night clothes on—most of them were bare-footed—and there wasn't a scrap of food or a drop of water amongst them all. In fact, they had to trudge bare-footed that month of November across those open marshes to Trepassey, where they were taken by schooners to the capital city of St. John's.

And perhaps the most amazing thing about the whole business was the fact that up on this rock, 100 feet above the level of the raging sea, while as yet most of the survivors were still aboard the doomed ship, the wife of a Sergeant of the Royal Veteran Battalion gave birth to a new-born infant—and, what's more amazing still, both she and her infant child eventually reached St. John's where they got a vessel bound to her home in England.

The Miraculous Rescue of The *Eric's* Crew

September 1940

Do you believe in Providence—or rather do you believe in the active intervention of Providence in the affairs of men? Or, to put it bluntly, do you believe in miracles? Whatever your views, it's hard to know the story of the brigantine Eric and not believe in miracles—for if ever men were snatched from the jaws of death it was surely the crew of that vessel. All around Bonavista, Elliston and Catalina they still talk—talk with bated breath—of that miraculous escape.

The brigantine hailed from Carbonear, where she was owned by Rorke and Sons. In the spring of 1878 her owners decided to send her to the icefields in search for seals. Under command of Captain Perry and carrying a crew of sixty-four sealers and seamen, she slipped away from Carbonear on the fifth of March. She had plain sailing until the ninth, when the first misfortune overtook them. One of the men broke his leg. Then on the twenty-second of the month, as all the men were out on the ice taking seals, they were overtaken by a hurricane of wind and snow.

For the next thirty hours they went through a terrible time, and two of them never got back to the vessel—it was presumed that they'd fallen through the ice. Fifteen of the men were very badly frost-bitten and hardly a man escaped uninjured or unaffected by those terrible thirty hours of exposure. In fact, the effect upon their health was so bad that Captain Perry saw the uselessness of remaining out much longer, and on the twenty-fifth he put the brigantine about and started back for Carbonear.

He must have been well down north, for we read that on the second of April he bespoke the steamer *Eagle*, and from her obtained their true position and the correct course for land. That was a Tuesday.

It was on the following Friday that they ran into the beginning of the disaster that overtook them.

It must have been snowing pretty thickly at the time, for suddenly the dread cry rang out from the man on look-out "Breakers ahead!" They were practically up on the breakers before seeing them—they didn't know it then, but they were just off the settlement of Bird Island Cove, a few miles south of Cape Bonavista, on the northern side of Trinity Bay. (Bird Island Cove, incidentally, has since been renamed Elliston, in honour of the Rev. William Ellis, one of the earliest of Methodist ministers there).

The brigantine was nearly up on the breakers when the warning came, and Captain Perry shouted a swift order to let go both anchors. Reaching bottom, the anchors brought up, just in time—for had she actually gone up on those terrible rocks it's more than doubtful if a solitary man would have lived to tell the tale. So here they were, lying at double-anchor in a violent sea and a swirling snow-storm, a matter of yards only from one of the worst breakers clear around the Newfoundland coast—sixty-three human beings with nothing between them and death but the storm buffeted brigantine, and she threatening every moment to carry them

16

all to their doom. The wind, which blew direct from the south-east, continued to increase in violence.

Try to picture that awful Friday night, as the hours and minutes dragged along and daylight finally broke—you can well believe that it was indeed a night of terror.

On Saturday Captain Perry saw that as things stood there wasn't a hope for any of them—the brigantine simply couldn't live in that sea; at any moment the anchors would drag or the chains break or something else would happen to send her crashing onto the rocks. He ordered the masts to be cut away to lighten the ship, make her more buoyant, and so enable her rather more easily to ride out the storm. All the time the storm rose in intensity, and great seas pounded her relentlessly. The sixty-three men huddled behind what shelter they could find on deck, expecting every moment to be their last.

On shore the high cliffs were lined with people from Elliston, and from Bonavista, five miles from there, and Catalina, ten miles away on the other side. They were completely helpless—no boat in the world would live a minute in that awful sea. There they were all day Saturday, and again all through that Saturday night, with the storm continuing with not a bit less violence and the brigantine straining and groaning under the impact of one tremendous sea after another.

Knowing so well the character of those rocks and that shore, the people on the cliffs had even less hope for the men aboard the brigantine than the men had themselves. At any moment they expected to see the vessel founder or be swamped, or break clear and be smashed upon the rocks—and her crew be hurled to their doom into the boiling mad sea. In full expectation of that happening, the anxious watchers ashore made what preparations they could by gathering coils of rope, ladders, boat-hooks, life-buoys and so forth—their thought being that when the ship was smashed up and the men were hurled into the water, by great good luck a few of them might get past the worst of the sea inside into calmer water, within reach of the ropes and life-buoys. And so that long Saturday passed interminably away, and darkness fell.

Now began the worst of it—that endless night of darkness in the howling storm, with absolutely nothing to cheer those aboard but the flickering fire made on the cliffs and kept burning by the watchers ashore to let the seamen know that human beings were there ready to give any help they could if occasion arose. But how could such an occasion arise if the ship met her doom before dawn? They'd die like rats in a trap. At last the first faint streaks of dawn lighted the sky, and now with the seas running fiercer than ever from several days' unceasing wind their position was worse than ever.

Practically every man aboard the *Eric* gave up the last flickering spark of hope. The minutes passed, then the hours. On the cliffs ashore the watchers whispered prayers for the souls of the doomed seamen aboard the brigantine. It seemed to be the end.

But suddenly there's a shout—a shout of joy and astonishment and in-credulity all mixed together—the shouter points to sea—the others look, and a cheer breaks from their throats. Aboard the brigantine, too, a man happened to look seaward—at first his brain refused to believe what his eyes see—then

17

something snaps inside him and he gives a hoarse shout. The others follow his gaze, and a cheer breaks from them.

It was the miracle!

No, not another ship—another ship would have been just as helpless in that spot as the *Eric* herself. It was a pale, low-lying narrow strip of something on the water—a long narrow strip of ice! And it was coming steadily toward them. It must have been nearly half a mile in length and perhaps a hundred yards or perhaps less in width—but it was salvation. Every minute that passed brought it nearer and nearer—at last the first of this providential strip of ice was actually up to the brigantine, brushing against her bows, being pushed and guided by the men past her and in toward the shore.

Yes, what had come was a bridge!—a floating bridge of ice that would connect vessel to shore.

Waiting not a second longer than long enough to see that the miraculous strip of ice was actually moving in toward the shore, twenty of the men left the brigantine instantly, got on the ice, went in to the inner end of it, and then waited for the ice to reach the shore. Men, under the leadership of High Constable McGowan, who was then stationed at Catalina and was afterwards so well known in St. John's, a party of Elliston and Bonavista men climbed down the perilous cliffs with their ropes and gaffs, and stood waiting for the men to get near enough to be hauled up over the cliff to the top to safety....

Well, the rest is very briefly told. Those twenty men were rescued, and all the rest of the *Eric's* crew were rescued, and the only casualty was to the man named Oldford, who had his leg broken in the rescue work. Conspicuous for his bravery on that memorable occasion was Arthur Tilley, and also Constable Bailey of Bonavista—but it's perhaps invidious to single out any two or three—all the rescuers were brave men, as only Newfoundland fishermen know how to be brave along the storm-tossed shores of Newfoundland....That's the story of the providential escape of the sixty-three men aboard the brigantine *Eric* of Carbonear—after reading of it don't you agree that it was providential, truly a modern miracle?

* * *

Trying Experience

February 1939

I've got a story to tell you now that is going to occupy the rest of my time for tonight, and my only regret is that I haven't taken the entire time of this broadcast to relate it, because it's one of the most remarkable Newfoundland stories I've come across yet. And it's sent to me by the only living survivor of the events to be described—Mr. James F. Kennedy, of Lake View, Hr. Main, who is now in his eighty-fifth year.

He was only thirteen years old when it happened, but you won't find it hard to believe, when you hear about it, that he remembers it today in all its grim details just as vividly as though it were only yesterday, whereas in fact it occurred in the Fall of the year 1866—just seventy-one years ago.

18

In that year he was one of a hundred and four men, women and children who were passengers aboard the Avondale brigantine *Damsel*, commanded by Captain Michael Costello, bound from Labrador to Conception Bay.

In those days the Labrador fishermen used to take their families with them to their fishing rooms along the Labrador coast, and the *Damsel* on this occasion was bringing over 100 fishermen and women and children back in the Fall with a Summer's fishing.

They left Dark Tickle on November 3rd, and at two o'clock in the morning of the 5th, in a terrible gale from the North-East, thick snow and a fierce sea, she ran on a reef in one of the worst places on the entire coast of Newfoundland— no less a place than the middle bill of the fearsome Cape Freels at the northernmost tip of Bonavista Bay. I've seen this spot more than once myself, both from the sea and land, and a terrible sight it is in a mad sea. When the *Damsel* ran on this reef only a hundred and fifty fathoms from the shore it was pitch-black darkness, and practically nobody aboard was up or dressed but the members of the crew who were on watch.

Great seas began to sweep over the doomed ship the moment she struck, and the men, women and children rushed on deck in their night clothes—hardly a person aboard had his or her outer clothing on. Nobody knew where they were, not even the Captain or other Officers. Some thought they'd run ashore at the Funks, others the Wadham Islands. All the boats but two were soon dashed to pieces or carried away, and in this pitiful plight the 104 souls aboard clung to the rigging on deck until the break of dawn when the Captain called for volunteers to try to launch a boat and make for shore.

The first boat that landed was smashed up on the rocks the moment its occupants landed, and then more volunteers were asked to man the remaining boat to carry a line ashore. Three men managed to get a line from the schooner to the rocks, and by means of this a five-inch hawser was hauled in and made fast. By this means, the sea having moderated somewhat, all the passengers were got ashore, two and three at a time, in their half-naked condition, my informant, Mr. Kennedy, then a thirteen-year-old boy, having to look out for himself.

But the plight of this thirteen-year-old lad, bad as it was, was a mere picnic compared with the terrible plight of one other passenger who happened to be aboard the illfated brigantine. This was Mrs. Costello, wife of the Captain's brother. Just a little more than an hour before the *Damsel* brigantine struck the reef in the raging gale, Mrs. Costello had become the mother of a new baby boy. And you can imagine the eagerness with which everybody aboard, in spite of the terrible peril to their own lives, co-operated gladly, with true Newfoundland courage, in scraping up some warm clothing and assistance to Mrs. Costello and her brand new baby boy, in that awful time. Says Mr. Kennedy, in writing me the story from Hr. Main, "If water is any good to baptize a child, he was baptized with millions of gallons."

From daylight until well up in the forenoon, it took the herculean efforts of the sweating men with only the one small boat to land all the passengers from the ship. And when they landed 'twas only to a narrow strip of rocky, snow-covered ground completely out of sight of house or habitation—and still they had no idea of where they were.

About two o-clock that day a man who was bound from Cape Freels to Cat Hr., now known as Lumsden, happened to pass that way and saw the shivering survivors—a number had been drowned that awful night and morning, and others had died of exposure. After making a fire with some gun-powder he had with him, this man hurried back to Cape Freels, which was only a little more than two miles away. As soon as they heard the news the kindly people of Cape Freels rushed to the scene of the disaster, and as they'd brought no extra clothes with the, they stripped themselves all but naked to give clothing to the women and children. Stretchers were hastily rigged up and the women and children carried over the snow-covered ground to the settlement, and then on the Pool's Island and Greenspond, where a small steamer carried them to their homes.

The baby boy born on that memorable night aboard the brigantine *Damsel* not only lived to tell the tale, but died in 1928 at the age of sixty-two, leaving a family who live in Avondale today. How I'd like to have the pleasure of meeting with Mr. Kennedy himself, and hearing from the lips of the only living survivor of that terrible occasion, all the details of the wreck of the brigantine *Damsel*.

* * *

<h2 style="text-align:center">Seventeen Terrible Days at Sea</h2>

August 1940

It is doubtful if very many Newfoundland seamen ever had a harder time or endured greater hardships than did the crew of the schooner Rigel on her way from Sydney, N.S. to Harbour Grace in the fall and winter of 1913. That voyage of the Rigel is an object lesson in the sort of thing that can happen to make a life on the sea one of terror and peril.

With a crew consisting of Capt. S.C. Mayo, Mate Berkley Breen, Seamen W. Blagdon, B. Brady and George Lee, and cook W. Moshur, all of them belonging to Fortune on the south-west coast, the schooner left Sydney with a load of coal late in the month of December, 1911. They encountered bad weather from the first day out, and were forced three days later to put into St. Pierre for shelter, and then again, after leaving St. Pierre, into Burin again for shelter, getting in there on Christmas Day and remaining till the 26th of the month. By ten o'clock on the night of the 27th they were passing by the Narrows on their way to Harbour Grace, but as the wind was unfavourable Captain Mayo decided to put in here for shelter till the wind was favourable.

They got into the very entrance to the Narrows, and could see the welcoming lights of St. John's, when suddenly the wind veered and blew a regular hurricane.

The schooner was blown for miles and miles away from the Narrows, and never in his twenty-five years on the sea did the captain experience such a night of wild terror as he did that night. Great seas swept her from stem to stern, and her jib and jumbo were blown away in shreds. By daylight next morning the storm increased in violence, and they discovered that they were ten miles off from Cape

Race. Out there a huge comber swept over her deck, smashing her boat to splinters, carrying away her deckhouse, tearing off the forecastle slides, and battering the bulwarks on the starboard side. Last. but not least their water-boat was splintered, so that they lost most of their drinking water.

On Sunday the wind veered to the northwest, and the seas continued all day to sweep over her, so that it seemed a physical impossibility for her to survive the terrific pounding or for men to live aboard her. Then she started to leak. It was all hands to the pumps—but to work the pumps the men had to lash themselves to them to keep from being swept overboard by the seas which came aboard.

One of the members of the crew, George Lee, was only a lad, making his first voyage. One mighty sea, sweeping over her, carried him off—but with the crazy freakishness of the ocean swept him back onto the deck, and he was able to scramble back to safety and lash himself onto something solid.

All day Sunday and again on Monday the storm raged with hurricane force, but by midnight Monday both the wind and sea slackened somewhat, and they availed of the comparative lull to set a trysail as a jib, to try to reach in toward the land. By midnight Tuesday, twenty-four hours later, they could see the light on Bay Bulls Head. Their troubles seemed to be over at least—but then a very thick snowstorm sprang up, the wind increased again, and they were carried twenty-two miles to sea.

By midnight on Wednesday there was some let-up in the storm again, though it was still too violent to attempt to make sail. And now the water began to gain fast on them—since Saturday they'd been at the pumps almost continuously, with scarcely an hour's sleep—and though some fifteen tons of coal which she'd been carrying on her deck had been swept away by the seas, it was felt that the schooner was still too deep, so they began feverishly to jettison some of the cargo, taking it out of the for'ard part, and letting her nose rise up out of the water. This was no sooner done, and she was riding a bit more buoyantly, then the temperature dropped swiftly and it began to freeze bitterly. Ice began to form all over the schooner, and all hands had to take axes and hatchets to cut away the ice as it formed so as to lighten ship. This wasn't bad enough, and next thing they knew they'd lost their log.

By daylight next day, Thursday, their position looked hopeless in the extreme—it seemed as though human flesh and blood couldn't stand any more. For the best part of a whole week the little crew of men had gone sleepless, almost without food, as they slaved and toiled day and night for days on end in their desperate battle to get into the shelter of land and into a harbour out of that wicked storm.

And then suddenly it was noticed that the water seeping into her was no longer making any headway, and they discovered to their delight that it was stopped by the coal dust, which had become thick and caky with water and formed a paste which got into the leaky seams and kept the water out. But the freezing weather continued, and the men dared not stop for a minute cutting the ice away as it formed on the vessel's hull, almost every inch of the hull above the water line.

And thus, for five days more, the schooner wallowed in that long-drawn-out storm in sub-zero weather—for five whole days and nights more the five men and one boy wondered if ever again they'd see land or human creature.

They were almost in their last gasp, when it almost seemed as well to die and be out of their misery as to live, a sail was sighted. They were then forty-two miles east-south-east of Cape Race. They made frantic signals to the oncoming vessel, and the *Gaspe*, Captain Connors, as it proved to be, bore down upon them to see what the trouble was. In the mad sea 'twas no easy job to transfer from their own vessel to the *Gaspe*, but the transfer was made, Captain Mayo as a last act overturning the stove in the cabin and setting fire to his doomed schooner. That was on the twelfth of January, and when at last they were safely aboard their rescuer they'd spent nearly seventeen days and nights battling for their very lives against the most terrible storm any of them had ever experienced in their entire seagoing lives.

A great big sea

The Ship That Went Nowhere Fast

January 1940

Is there anybody living today who was a member of the whaling ship Puma in the year 1903 up in Placentia Bay? There was one trip the whaler made around Placentia Bay that nobody aboard her at the time will ever forget to his dying day.

It happened one day, not far off Placentia, the ship's crew harpooned a great sulphur-bottom whale. The harpoon missed the vital part of the whale, but entered about fifteen feet from the great mammal's tail. The immense whale immediately started ahead, and though the steamer's engines were put full speed astern the whale towed her ahead at the speed of ten knots an hour. The skipper ordered a block placed under the harpoon-line, with a man standing by with an axe ready to cut the line should there be any danger of the ship's being dragged under.

At the speed of ten knots the great whale continued in an almost straight distance across the bay of fifty-two miles, quite near the Burin light. The whale then turned at right angles, still towing the steamer, and crossed the Bay again to St. Mary's, a distance of forty-two miles. Here the whale turned again and ran toward Red Island, but now the great mammal's strength had lessened considerably, and the speed had dropped a lot below ten knots, so that by the time Red Island, twenty-five miles away, was reached, the whale was quite spent, and gave up the uneven fight. The crew put another harpoon into the huge body, and the battle was over. For twenty-six hours the ship was in tow of the whale, during which she was towed a total distance of a hundred and twenty-two miles in zig-zag fashion around Placentia Bay—surely one of the queerest experiences that ever befell a ship in Newfoundland or any other waters.

PIRATES

Pike, The Pirate

April 1940

One of the most famous characters ever produced in Newfoundland, was a man named Pike who was born in Carbonear. He was born somewhere in the 1780's or even a few years earlier. As a young fellow he emigrated to the United States in search of work. He wasn't up there very long before he entered the American navy, where his experience, ability and contempt of danger won him pretty quick promotion. In the war of 1814, as you probably know, Newfoundland waters were infested with American privateersmen—little better than pirates, if any better— and the most notorious of all these privateersmen was the Newfoundlander, Pike. His exploits became famous. The American privateersmen generally weren't a bit particular as to whether the ships they attacked were English or Newfoundland— 'twas all one to them. With Pike, however, it made all the difference in the world. He inflicted terrible damage on English shipping, but he was never known to attack or molest a Newfoundland-owned vessel. In fact, whenever he knew a vessel to be a Newfoundland boat, and the crew to be Newfoundlanders, he went out of his way to show his partiality—he not only refused to attack them, and let them go, but pressed food luxuries upon them. Pike was a sort of second John Paul Jones in the American Navy. There are a number of Pikes living in Carbonear. Have any of them any records and traditions or information of any sort about this famous Carbonear man?

* * *

The Lady and The Pirates

January 1940

I'm indebted to Mrs. Doctor V.P. Burke for this amazingly interesting pirate story of old-time Newfoundland. It concerns a Newfoundland woman named Lucretia Parker, and whether Lucretia Parker has any descendants living in this country today, or whether any descendants of the same family are living here now, I'm afraid I can't say. This story occurred in the year 1825, only 115 years ago, so it could be that Lucretia was the great-grandmother of some of the present-day generation of Parkers.

It seems that one of her brothers, Thomas Parker, had purchased a plantation and was making his home in Antigua, one of the more southerly of the West Indian Islands. He wrote to his sister Lucretia in St. John's, where she was living, and where in all probability he had previously been living himself, asking her to take passage to Antigua to live with him and his wife. And accordingly, on the twenty-eight of February, 1825, Miss Parker took passage aboard the sloop *Eliza Ann*, whose captain was a man named Charles Smith.

They had a favourable wind from the time they left Newfoundland, and it looked as though the trip were going to prove quite a humdrum and uneventful

24

one. Little did Captain Smith and his men dream that they were on their last voyage—that never again would they set eyes on Newfoundland—that within a fortnight they would all be dead.

For on the fourteenth day out from St. John's they sighted a small schooner standing toward them, with her deck swarming with men. They knew at once that it was a pirate ship. The pirate ship ran up alongside them, and in an instant the deck of the sloop was crowded with blood-thirsty cut-throats armed with pistols, cutlasses and knives. Without ceremony the pirates fell on the sloop's small crew, and the scene was a bedlam of curses and blows.

Lucretia Parker fell on her knees and began to pray. From the one pirate who seemed to be master of the others she begged for mercy—begged to have her life spared. The pirate captain heeded her pleas, and led her to the companionway and ordered her below into the cabin, and locked the door of the companionway behind her. From her position in the cabin she could hear the shouts and curses on deck, and concluded that the crew of the *Eliza Ann* were being butchered by the buccaneers.

After she had been there for more than an hour the noise died down, and then the door of the companionway opened and down came eight or ten of the pirates, led by their captain, pouring into the cabin. But they were only looking for the money they supposed the captain of the sloop had hidden there—they made no move whatever to molest their female captive. Then the pirates returned to the deck and, leaving so many aboard to sail the sloop, went back to their own schooner.

Lucretia Parker had no idea of what was happening, or whither the two vessels were bound, till at length they arrived at a small island which proved to be the pirates' rendezvous. Then she learned that the captain and crew of the *Eliza Ann* had not been murdered, for when the sloop's hatches were removed the men came up on deck in response to the pirate captain's order. They had been in the hold of the sloop all the time. But it was not in the pirates' minds to spare them—far from it. As soon as they had all landed on the island the brutal buccaneers began to torture the men. Captain Smith was killed instantly with a knife thrust. Others were killed with blows from clubs. Lucretia Parker was forced to look on while the entire crew of the sloop was butchered. Then she was taken into a shack and locked in.

On the following morning the pirate captain appeared in the cabin. He was nearly six feet in height, of a swarthy complexion, with black and penetrating eyes—she never learned his nationality, but it was plain to see that all the pirates—there were forty of them—stood in considerable awe of him. At sight of him she fell on her knees and began to pray again, and after gazing intently at her he left the shack again. She spent a terribly uneasy day and night, and on the following morning the pirate chief again visited her. But he had no sooner entered the shack than there was the sound of a bugle-call. It was the signal from the pirate stationed on the look-out that there was a sail in sight, and instantly the captain turned about and left again. Mustering up her courage, Lucretia Parker stood up on a box to peer through the window, and a glad sight it was that greeted her eyes. A short distance from the island she spied a vessel which appeared to be lying to, and a few miles to windward of her another, which appeared to be bearing down toward her under press of sail. She hoped it might mean rescue—and the pirates, who knew what the two ships were, began a feverish activity. All but four of them jumped into their small boats and rushed to get to their own schooner with a view to making their escape before the British warship could cut them off.

By the time, however, they had reached the schooner and begun to get her underway the two warships had opened fire on them. Some of them jumped into the water to swim ashore, but every man of them was captured and taken aboard the two British ships. But to her anguished disappointment they turned about and departed without coming on the island, and here she was left alone in the charge of the four pirates who still remained on the island.

Perhaps it was the fright they'd got from the appearance of the British warships, and the capture of their buddies, but at all events the four remaining pirates changed their attitude toward the Newfoundland girl, and they announced their intention of getting away from the island as quickly as they could, and to get her to some place of safety.

One of the four pirates was an Englishman, and he told her his story, claiming that he had been forced into piracy. He told her that the pirate band had captured and plundered dozens of vessels—the plunder they'd sent to somebody on one of the populated islands of the West Indies to sell for them. Once their decision to leave the island was taken, the four men set about demolishing the remaining shacks, and then dug up a hole in the earth from which they took several bags of money, which they put aboard their boat. Then they took her with them and set sail. About midnight they landed her on the shore of another island, which they told her was Cuba, gave her some water and hard biscuit, and directions as to what direction to take when she landed.

That was the last she ever saw or heard of them, and to make a long story short she followed their instructions and came to an isolated house, whose occupants she guessed were friends of the pirates, and the man of this house took her to the Cuban town of Mantansies, where she found many Americans and Europeans. She struck passage on a vessel bound to Jamaica, and in Jamaica, where she was treated with the greatest possible kindness and consideration by the Governor and officials, she had the last installment of her thrilling and gruesome adventure. She discovered that the thirty-six pirates captured by the two British warships had been brought here, and were then lying in jail awaiting trial! She was asked to accompany the officials to the prison to see if she could identify them. She recognized the pirate captain and most of the others, and through her evidence they were all sentenced—seven of them to execution by hanging, the others to various other forms of punishment. Lucretia Parker was invited by the Governor to stay and witness the execution of the seven condemned men—they had queer ideas about hanging in those old days—but she'd had enough horror to last her a lifetime, and she firmly declined.

After spending nine days in Jamaica she was lucky enough to obtain a passage with a Captain Ellsmore direct to St. John's, where she arrived back safe and sound after one of the most thrilling and adventurous experiences it has ever been the fate of a woman to undergo in Newfoundland or any other country.

Lucretia Parker afterwards wrote the story of her adventures while a captive of the pirate gang, and published it as a pamphlet, and all the facts given have been compiled from that publication.

* * *

The Pirate Raid on Trepassey

July 1940

Of all the devastating raids ever made by pirates upon New-foundland—and there were a good many—one of the worst was the invasion of Trepassey Harbour by the notorious Captain Bartholomew Roberts in the summer of 1722, two hundred and eighteen years ago. Captain Roberts was an Englishman who, in the course of his sailor-ing, found himself in a West Indian port and signed on as second mate aboard a large vessel which he discovered, after they were at sea, to be a pirate ship. He ended up by becoming her captain, and then began one of the most amazing piratical careers ever recorded.

It is unknown how many times he visited Newfoundland—or indeed whether he ever made more than his one visit in 1722. Most of his time was spent along the Spanish Main, and it was after an encounter he had with two British sloops of war sent to capture him that he left those waters and sailed to Newfoundland.

Around the end of June he sailed into Trepassey with all his black colours flying, drums beating and trumpets sounding—it must have been a pretty fearsome sight to the unarmed fishermen of the place. Roberts burned and destroyed every one of the twenty-two vessels in the harbour at the time, with the exception of one Bristol galley, and never ceased his depredations till he'd destroyed all the small boats, stages and flakes of the settlement. The damage done that memorable day in Trepassey must have amounted to many thousands of dollars.

* * *

They Got the Treasure

November 1938

Amongst the people of Fogo District who are listening in tonight I wonder how many will remember the famous story of the foreign vessel that put into Shoal Bay in their district in 1897 and got away, according to tradition, with a buried treasure of considerable size?

A man named Thorne was one of a number of people who went in the year 1877 and settled in Shoal Bay—prior to that the place was quite uninhabited. Each family staked out a piece of land, and in the piece staked out by Thorne there was a mound of earth which he assumed to be the grave of some sailor or fishermen who had been buried there by a passing vessel. Thorne showed quite a bit of respect towards this mound, and he even went to the trouble of fencing it around. From 1877 until 1897 he kept this fence in good repair.

In the latter year this strange vessel put into the cove and dropped her anchor. That was about mid-day. Some of the fishermen rowed out to her with a view to

27

going aboard and learning who they were. The men aboard the vessel extended a very poor welcome to them, however, and when they were allowed aboard they were given orders by the vessel's captain not to go aft of the mainmast. One of the fishermen, however, managed to sneak aft and get a peep in the cabin. He was considerably impressed to see in the cabin a veritable arsenal of guns and ammunition. Then he was discovered and they were all driven off the ship.

The vessel remained in the harbour all that day and that night—but by daylight the following day she was gone again and from that day to this no word was ever heard of her. And Thorne, as well as the rest of the settlement, was astonished to find that the mound in his garden was no longer there—where the mound had been there was now only a gaping hole—the conclusion being irresistible that in the dead of night the crew of the foreign vessel had come ashore, dug open the mound, and removed whatever was in it.

STAGS, SALMON AND TUNA FISH

An Awful Fright

September 1938

If Mr. Josiah Sheppard, of Lark Harbour, Bay of Islands, is still living, I'm quite sure he hasn't forgotten the awful fright he once got while he was outside Lark Harbour on a fishing trip with his two brothers. I've often been in Lark Harbour, and I knew all the people there—and there was a Josiah Sheppard in my time, but I can't say if it's the same man, or a son.

This thing happened in 1912. One early morning in August of that year he left in a dory to go fishing. His brother Henry had a motorboat, so he got a tow out to the fishing grounds. After fishing for a while off Wee Bauld, Josiah had got only half a quintal of fish, so he and his brother Henry decided to take up their grapnels and move to another ground. Josiah got aboard his brother's motorboat till they reached the new ground. Then he got back in the dory, and Henry slacked the line till the dory drifted about 200 yards astern.

Josiah was just preparing to get out his lines for some hand-line fishing, when this thing happened. Up out of the water immediately beside his boat rose a huge monster of the deep—a cuttle-fish or octopus, several of which have been seen and even captured in Newfoundland waters in years gone by. This was altogether a huge monster, and its appearance was as quick as it was unexpected.

It reared its head up high out of the water, and in over the side of the dory. It looked intently at Sheppard, and then at the codfish in the bottom of the dory. Then, with one of its great tentacles, it seized the dory, and disappeared underneath the surface of the water with it. Sheppard was thrown in the water, but managed to give a terrific yell, as he felt himself going to attract his brothers' attention. As he was floundering about in the water the dory suddenly came to the surface again, bottom up. Sheppard managed to climb up on the bottom of the dory, where he waited until his two brothers came to his rescue.

Sheppard described the devil-fish as having a dreadful mouth of four feet across. In the side of the dory was the marks of the monster's bite, measuring about two and a half feet in size. The devil-fish had a white belly and a black back. Sheppard believed that it was only the presence of the half quintal of codfish on the bottom of the dory that saved his life. If the fish hadn't been there, he was always convinced that the devil-fish would have attacked him instead. And I myself am strongly inclined to agree with him.

Wrestled With Stag

October 1938

For some time past I have been promising myself the pleasure of calling upon Mr. Mark Gibbons, for some years past a resident of St. John's, to try to persuade him to relate some of his amazing adventures in various parts of this country. One of these days I hope to get around to it.

In the meantime here's one that I didn't get from Mr. Gibbons himself, and it's certainly well worth telling. This happened on the 15th of October, 1920, out at Stephenville Crossing, on the West Coast. Mr. Gibbons, who was on a prospecting trip I think, was passing through Stephenville Crossing at dawn that day.

As he passed along the road he noticed a herd of cattle, and the unusual sight of a big stag caribou standing amidst the cattle. The herd was quite near the road, and Mr. Gibbons had to pass them. Knowing also that as a rule stags don't attack men without good cause, he wasn't unduly worried by the presence of the caribou, though somewhat intrigued by his mixing with ordinary cattle.

Suddenly, just as he was passing the herd, this big 500 pound stag came charging toward him. Knowing from past experience the fighting habits of the stag, Mr. Gibbons waited till the stag was nearly upon him, and then dodged the charge, and in the same moment gripped the animal by his large antlers.

Then began what was quite literally a death struggle between the man and the beast. At no time did Mr. Gibbons give up his grip on the stag's antlers. Several times he had the stag down, and several times the stag had him down. This went on for quite some time, until Mr. Gibbons began to feel his own strength giving out. At the first opportune moment, therefore, he released his grip and ran toward a high fence on the side of the road. Quickly he climbed over this fence to the other

PANL A7-21

Stag Caribou

30

side, but almost as quickly the stag charged after him and bounded over the fence too.

Mr. Gibbons then scrambled back over the fence again, but the stag was after him in a flash, and he had to turn and face the infuriated animal again and grasp him by the antlers once more, when the struggle began all over again. The stag had succeeded in getting Mr. Gibbons down and was preparing to kill him with his antlers, when suddenly a young steer left the herd of cattle and charged full-speed at the stag, catching the caribou in his side with his sharp horns.

Instantly the stag turned on the steer, and a new fight was on. Mr. Gibbons took advantage of this new development to run as fast as his exhausted condition would permit to a nearby farm house. There he seized a rifle, and returned to the scene of the new battle. But at sight of him with the rifle, the stag bounded away. Mr. Gibbons gave chase and with two shots brought the animal down forever.

Mr. Gibbons was black and blue with bruises and injuries received in his fight with the huge stag, and had to receive treatment from Dr. R.J. Macdonald. Few men in Newfoundland have had the number and variety of experiences and adventures that Mr. Gibbons has known in his adventurous lifetime. (Since this broadcast Mr. Gibbons has passed away).

* * *

Rode a Moose

June 1940

Here's an item from Western Newfoundland, the sender being Mr. Leonard P. Moss of Deer Lake. It tells of a free ride on a wild bull moose. Mr. Moss says that this bull moose happened to stray into the landing ground where the winter haul of pulpwood was being landed in preparation for the spring drive. There were lots of dogs around at the time—dogs that were being used in hauling wood—and the moment the bull moose appeared the dogs tore toward him, surrounded him and barked and jumped around furiously, so that the moose was temporarily mesmerized and didn't see, or certainly didn't pay any attention to, the men who were there.

Amongst the men was George Rose, one of the daredevils of Deer Lake. Rushing in through the surrounding circle of dogs he sprang up over the moose's rump to his back, sitting astride. With that another man struck the moose with a switch, and the startled bull gave a spring and dashed off through the trees with George holding on for dear life.

The bull moose was travelling far too fast for him to jump off, and he was carried a distance of perhaps a quarter of a mile before the moose, passing underneath a projecting limb of a tree, swept him off his back and dashed away to freedom, leaving George Rose gasping for breath on the ground.

Rode Astride a Tuna Fish

February 1940

Mr. Richard T. Cook, of Cartyville, West Coast, says that back in 1888, a few years before the railway was put through out there, only a very little agriculture was carried on out that way—most of the people made their living at the fishery.

One spring somebody reported that the caplin had struck in at the Highlands, about eight miles away. About ten o'clock that night all the fishermen took their boats and started off to get caplin for bait. Mr. Cook, then a boy of fourteen, was taken along with his father. When they got there they found it was a false alarm—there were no caplin. It was a lovely calm morning, the water as smooth as glass.

They were just getting ready to turn back again when somebody shouted: "Look! horse mackerel—look at them jumping!" Of course horse mackerel is the Newfoundland fishermen's name for tuna fish.

A short distance from the shore there they were—a big school of the tuna fish, diving and sporting in the water. Hurriedly the men loaded their boats with fairly large stones from the beach and pulled for dear life on the oars. They rowed out fan-wise, to get outside of the school of fish and to form a sort of flank on both sides of them. Then they began throwing the stones for all their worth at the tuna fish—the idea was to frighten the fish and make them stampede toward the beach. And that's exactly what happened—by flinging the rocks, splashing the water with their oars and shouting they kicked up a fearful din, and the tuna fish were forced in toward the shoal water off the beach.

Squeezed in tight against each other, the big fish began to splash and jump and dive. One of the fishermen in the boats was a Scotsman named John Gillis—he was in a boat with his brother Alex Gillis. John Gillis was poised up on the stem of the boat, and in the excitement, as one big tuna came up out of the water Gillis leaped clear onto his back, sitting astride and holding for dear life to the fish's fins, one in each hand. The startled tuna immediately began to dive and jump, and then dived clear under the water, with Gillis holding on for dear life. Then he came to the surface again, just long enough for both fish and man to take a deep breath, and dived again.

The fishermen in the surrounding boats were at first paralysed with astonishment at the unheard-of daring and recklessness of John Gillis, but when they recovered they closed in upon the tuna and began striking it with their oars and boat-hooks till they had him out of commission.

Labrador's Sea-Monster

October 1940

From Rigolet, on the coast of Labrador, Mr. George Budgell of the Hudson's Bay Company trading post there writes to describe a sea-monster he once saw. Generally, whenever one is reported the whole world scoffs at it, with the plain suggestion that the sea-monsters existed only in the imagination of those who reported seeing them. However Mr. Budgell tells his story very well, so here it is:

"A few days ago, he says, I picked up an old magazine from a pile lying on the table, and the first thing that caught my eye was an account of a monster that had been seen somewhere in the United States. Well, I am going to tell you a true story of some kind of monster that was seen at this place three summers ago by myself and by at least two other men of the place. It happened this way: we had our little schooner, the *Fort Rigolet*, tied up to the wharf and were loading her with supplies for our North West River post. The tide was dead low, and you perhaps know that at low tide here the water rushes out through this narrow part of Gros Water Bay at the rate of about five or six knots, especially at spring tides; and it was about the height of the springs at that particular time.

"Anyway, I happened to look seawards, and I saw what appeared to be a huge black log floating down with the tide, about five hundred yards from the shore. Suddenly it lifted its head, and stared right at us with a pair of enormous sunken eyes that looked deadly human. The head would be about the size of the head of a square-flipper seal, and the neck I would judge to be at least fifteen or eighteen inches long. After staring at us for a matter of about fifteen seconds, it dived. During the process of diving it exposed three parts of its body (or as we say here, it humped its back when diving)—first the shoulders, then about the middle part of its body, and lastly its hinder part.

"I would judge it to have been at least fifteen feet long, and I would judge its body to have been as large as a pork barrel round the middle. If ever I put up an earnest prayer during my sinful career it was then that I might have my rifle by me at that moment. It has never since been seen in the locality or in any other locality so far as I can discover, but it was seen here at the time I mention by my son Leonard who was working in another part of our buildings at the moment; by John Blake, skipper of our motor vessel *Rigolet* who was standing by my side at the time; and myself. Both these men can corroborate my story."

33

Is This A Record?

April 1939

A correspondent in the city who signs his initials "A.E.W." writes to claim that he holds the record of taking longer to land a salmon than any other man in history. It happened at Pinsent's Falls, Salmonier, some years ago. He hooked this salmon at five o'clock in the morning, but it wasn't until seven o'clock that evening that he landed it.

What happened was this: the salmon, a few minutes after he was hooked, jumped up over the falls. The man who tells the story couldn't get up over the falls, as the trees grew close to the side all the way up. So he could only let the reel spin, and give the salmon the full length of line. It ended by his line snapping.

Shortly before seven that night he was fishing again, this time above the falls, and saw his line floating on the water. He managed to secure the end of it and then carefully threaded it through the eyes of his rod and attached it to the reel. Next minute there was a splash upstream, and the fight was on. He landed the salmon—a fine large one—at seven o'clock.

* * *

PANL B19-165

Looking for the big one

34

How Mrs. Peddle Caught a Tuna Fish

July 1939

Dan Benson writes in from Rantem, Trinity Bay, to tell of the unusual and plucky performance of Mrs. Thomas Peddle.

Mrs. Peddle belongs to Chance Cove, but was spending some time at Rantem Harbour. The mouth of Rantem Harbour is about two hundred yards wide. One day a school of what our Newfoundland fishermen call horse mackerel—their proper name is Tuna Fish—came in on one side of the Harbour and went out again on the other side, where the water is quite shoal.

Mrs. Peddle was watching the big fish, and noticed that one of them was coming along quite near to the shore. She ran and caught a piece of rope, made a half-hitch in it, and ran out in the water to her arm-pits, from which position she threw the rope over the tuna fish's tail, jerked it tight, and then hurried back to the shore and wound the rope around a heavy tree growing near the edge of the water. This brought the big fish up standing, and of course in a moment the fish was in a rage of splashing and plunging.

Mrs. Peddle held on grimly to the rope, and as he weakened she gradually shortened the rope until she had him landed. The tuna fish was eleven feet long, seven feet on the round, and filled four barrels when cut up.

* * *

Two Unwelcome Visitors

October 1940

Here's a queer experience a vessel had on the Banks. It's about the Grand Bank vessel *Antoine Santos*, owned by Foote's firm. She was out on the Banks fishing, and as so often happens, the water was literally alive with sharks—hundred of them all about her. At the same time there was a heavy sea, and the *Antoine Santos* was rolling pretty heavily. Every now and then her rail would go under water, and tons of water would be shipped aboard. Here's how plentiful the sharks were: in one of the dips she took, she literally scooped up two live sharks, which were left stranded on her deck. They were in one of the seas she shipped, and of course got caught inside the bulwarks when the ship righted herself. One thing is certain: they did not decide to keep the sharks for pets.

* * *

Put This Squid On Your Hook

August 1939

Mr. Robert Skiffington writes in from Musgravetown, Bonavista Bay, to tell me of a large squid his uncle, Bill Greening, picked up on a point in Goose Bay Head. After he'd cut it up it filled eight puncheons, his two longest tentacles filling a puncheon each. This great squid was forty feet long. Lots of giant squid have been driven ashore or enmeshed in traps in Newfoundland waters.

A Salmon in Rabbit Snare

March 1940

Here's a story that was sent from English Harbour West in Fortune Bay, by Mr. Clyde Keeping—it's a corker. Mr. Keeping says that one day a man by the name of William Bishop was in the woods gathering firewood, when it occurred to him to set some rabbit snares. He set the snares here and there, and after he had set about twenty to his satisfaction he noticed a sort of beaten path that he thought might be a very good place to set one. He did so, and about a week or so later he was in there to take a look at his snares.

He got two or three rabbits out of the snares, and then he happened to think of the snare he'd set in this beaten path. He'd almost forgotten this snare, and was actually turning back to return home when he remembered it. He went to see the snare, and what do you think he found in it?

Not a rabbit—not any sort of animal—but a salmon! Yes, sir—a three pound salmon.

It sounds unbelievable, but Mr. Keeping states it as a solemn fact. and after hearing his explanation you'll see that it's quite probably the naked truth. The path where he set this snare was one which ran to the bank of a river, and he set the snare quite near the bank of the river. During the week that elapsed between the time when he set the snare and when he came back to look at it, there had been heavy rains, and the river overflowed its banks, covering the snare completely. This three-pound salmon had darted right through the snare and had got caught around the girth. Without a doubt that's the first time on record in this country, or any other country, when a salmon was captured in a rabbit snare.

* * *

He Put an Eel to Good Use

June 1940

Gregory John writes from Glenwood to relate a very ingenious method he devised to recover something he'd lost in a deep pool in the river. He was salmon fishing at Salmon Falls on the Gander River, when he accidentally dropped a valuable hunting knife to the bottom of a twenty-foot pool just below the falls. And how do you suppose he got it up again?

After trying with a hook and line and one or two other means, he finally hit on a really bright idea. First of all he caught an eel. Then very carefully he lowered the eel into the pool to the knife, which he could see sticking up by the point from the bottom—the eel coiled itself around the knife, Gregory John drew the eel to the surface again and there was his fine knife safe and sound again.

BELIEVE IT OR NOT

A Local Fire-Eater

November 1938

Well, ladies and gentlemen, yesterday afternoon I had a most interesting experience myself. And I didn't have to go looking for it—it came looking for me.

It all began on Saturday night, just after I finished my broadcast, when one of my listeners telephoned to ask if I had read an item in the local papers telling of a man somewhere or other who could actually, without injury to himself, lick a red-hot iron with his tongue. I said I hadn't read it, but what about it, anyway?

"Oh, nothing," he said, "except that right here in St. John's is a man I know who'll do the same thing."

"You mean to tell me," I said, "that you know a man here in the city who is prepared to lick a red-hot piece of iron with his tongue?"

My listener said yes, and undertook to bring this man down to my office so that I could see him do it.

And yesterday afternoon down he came, bringing this local fire-eater with him. The fire-eater's name is Stanley Short, and he lives at 254 New Gower Street. When I expressed absolute unbelief in his willingness and ability to perform this wonder, Stanley Short didn't attempt to argue the point, or to try by word of mouth to convince me.

He just asked very simply: "Have you got a poker or lifter?"

I gave him a short thick stove-lifter, and he poked one end in through the bars of the grate.

In less than ten minutes this lifter was blood-red hot on one end—so hot—that even the outside end couldn't be gripped until two handkerchiefs were wrapped around it. There was no fake about it—I saw it with my own eyes— another gentleman was in the office at the time and saw it with his own eyes.

Deliberately and slowly, while this gentleman and I watched in fascinated amazement, and a bit white about the gills, deliberately and slowly Stanley Short licked this glowing, blood-red hot lifter with his tongue—not once, not twice, but no less than four separate times within quarter of a minute.

You could hear his tongue sizzle every time he licked it. This other gentleman and myself were absolutely paralysed with astonishment, and when I regained sufficient strength to ask him if his tongue were burned, he replied "No," not hurt at all—here, I'll do it again."

But I had had enough for one day, and I'm authorised to tell you that if you don't believe this story, Stanley Short is quite cheerfully willing to perform the amazing stunt again, either in private or public for anyone who wants to see it done.

All of which goes to show you once again, ladies and gentlemen, that Newfoundlanders can lick anything that comes up against them.

* * *

A Local Genius

December 1938

Ladies and gentlemen, I think I'd be the very last man in the country to say a word to minimize the value and importance of a good education.

I hope you won't think that the story I'm going to tell you now is meant to show you that education is not needed. It is needed, and needed far more today than it was ever needed before.

But this story is about a Newfoundlander who didn't have a single scrap of education. He was never inside a school door. He couldn't write or read his own name. No pencil or pen was ever seen in his hand. And yet Theophilus Hart. of Lady Cove, Trinity Bay, was by all accounts absolutely a mathematical genius, and I cannot help wondering what he might have become had he only received a good education—probably another Albert Einstein or Bertrand Russell.

Ask him how many feet were in a piece of scantling 3½ by 4½ by 7½ feet long and he'd work it out in his head and give you the answer inside of a few moments. It didn't matter what were the dimensions of the piece of lumber, he'd give you the answer just the same.

Once he was aboard a Trinity Bay schooner loaded with lumber of all kinds and sizes. The lumber was consigned to no less than twenty three different people, and after it was all delivered and the vessel was empty the owner of the lumber, Mr. W.H. Gulliford, together with another man on the schooner, got out their paper and pencils and began to figure the thing out—how much money was coming to each of the twenty-three men.

Theophilus Hart, with no pencil or paper, began to figure the thing in his head. By two o'clock in the morning the two men with pencils and paper had arrived at their totals—Mr. Hart had got his totals quite a while before they did. And when they were all finished neither one's figure agreed with the other two—all three totals were different. So next morning the skipper called aboard a man from ashore, a competent accountant, who figured it all out for him, and what do you suppose?

The only man of the three who had figured it correctly was Theophilus Hart.

The correspondent who sends me this story tells me that the late Judge Johnson of the Supreme Court told him that he regarded Theophilus Hart as the smartest uneducated man in the world. On his political campaigns through Trinity Bay Judge Johnson had got to know Mr. Hart very well, and always stayed at Hart's house in Lady Cove, and when Mr. Hart came into St. John's he always stayed with Judge Johnson.

It makes me just a little sick to realize what a mathematical genius was probably lost to Newfoundland by the failure of Theophilus Hart to secure a good education.

* * *

When Bottles Carried World News

May 1940

You've doubtless noticed that a period of 11 years elapsed between the time when you could telegraph from Newfoundland to the mainland of America, and the time when you could send a cable across the Atlantic Ocean. Of course until the trans-Atlantic cable was landed and operating, the whole cable system was less than half as useful as it afterwards became.

Here's how they used to get over the difficulty created by the long gap between Newfoundland and Europe. Up at Cape Race there was a telegraph office at the end of a land-line cable from the Cape to St. John's. Steamships coming across the Atlantic would write messages intended for Canada or America, wrap them carefully in bottles or other watertight containers, and throw them overboard in the water near Cape Race.

Boats would put out from the Cape, the messages would be picked up out of the water and then sent over the land-line cable to the western tip of Newfoundland, and then by the submarine cable across the Cabot Strait. In exactly the same way steamships going across the Atlantic would pick up messages thrown overboard at Cape Race, and carry them over. It means, at least, that if you left New York for Europe, your last news of a personal or business character wouldn't end on the day your steamer sailed, but on the day she passed Cape Race.

The great daily newspapers of the United States paid large sums of money to have the latest news picked up at Cape Race from steamships coming across the Atlantic, and forwarded by cable from Cape Race days ahead of the steamships themselves. Even that was considered a marvellous achievement in those days, crude as it seems to us today who live in an age when a man stands before a radio microphone in London or Paris, and you can hear even his breathing on this side of the Atlantic.

* * *

Believe It or Not

October 1939

Here's one of the queerest of all the queer things that ever happened in connection with Newfoundland. Early in the eighteen hundreds an English vessel sailed out of the port of Poole, England, bound for Newfoundland. She was gone several months before she returned to Poole. And when she did return her captain reported that he had steered direct for Newfoundland, but could find no trace of it. He said he thought Newfoundland must have disappeared beneath the waves!

* * *

Our Mildest Winter

December 1939

What was the mildest winter we ever had in Newfoundland? Undoubtedly the winter of 1899. On the 11th of January that winter William Woodley, a farmer near Quidi Vidi, ploughed an acre of land on his farm, and all the farmers near St. John's were ploughing that day. Some of them top-dressed their fields. Hundreds of sheep were to be seen out in the fields grazing, and up to that time, and even later, not a scrap of their reserves of hay had been touched.

And then, on the twenty first of February, in Bannerman Park, a game of football was played, that there are people living in St. John's will remember to this very day, though it was nearly fifty years ago. Amongst the players were the late Hon. F.C. Alderdice, Andrew Thorburn, Joseph Peters, George Langmead and George Tessier. It isn't very often that football is played in the month of February, is it?

* * *

Caplin in October

July 1938

If you were to hear that caplin had struck in at any place in Newfoundland in the month of October, you'd surely say that such a thing was impossible. And yet up in Trepassey and other places along that shore, caplin once struck in, in fairly considerable quantities, as late as November 8.

Without a doubt there are lots of people living today who will confirm the statement. It happened in 1907. Some people may contend that it wasn't caplin, but white fish, that struck in at Trepassey—but I have no doubt that the fishermen of Trepassey who secured these caplin are just as capable of telling white fish from caplin as any other fisherman in the island.

* * *

Four Newfoundlands in the World

March 1940

Probably you'd be surprised to know that there are no less than five places in this world known by the name Newfoundland. This country of ours, in other words, isn't the only place that's called Newfoundland, though of course it's a million times the most important of the four places which bear the name. The second place called Newfoundland is Newfoundland, a village of Elliott County in the State of Kentucky, United States of America. Then there's a place called Newfoundland, a village of Morris County in the State of New Jersey, and Newfoundland Island, Labrador. And finally there's Newfoundland, a village in Wayne County, in the State of Pennsylvania.

HISTORICAL

Gov. Holloway's Wooing of the Beothucks

November 1940

Vice Admiral John Holloway, Governor of Newfoundland in the year 1805 was only one of several governors in the early part of last century who took a keen interest in the subject of the aborigines of Newfoundland, the Beothuck Indians. But Governor Holloway's particular way of showing his interest, or rather the particular scheme he worked out to win the friendship of the Beothucks, makes his name stand out from amongst the other Governors in a way that's quite pleasant to remember. Admiral Sir J.T. Duckworth and Sir Erasmus Gower were other Governors who devised schemes to make friends with the Indians, Duckworth being the man under whose authority Lieut. Buchan made his famous and tragic expedition into the interior. Governor Holloway's scheme was a very novel one. He proposed to win over the Indians with pictures.

His plan was outlined in a special dispatch he sent to Lord Castlereagh in London. Ever since Newfoundland had been visited and inhabited by white men, he pointed out, the Indians had been very shabbily treated. There were just a few exceptions, especially that of Sir Richard Whitbourne in the very early history of the country—he got on famously with the Beothucks. But on the whole our people treated the Indians shamefully—the aborigines were regarded as scarcely human, and it was considered quite proper to shoot them on sight. No wonder, then, that the Indians grew to be profoundly suspicious of the white man, and to look upon him as a bitter enemy.

And of course by their petty thieving propensities the Indians didn't exactly help their own cause—in their annual visits from the interior to the coast they used to steal the salmon out of the white men's nets and sometimes steal the food, not to speak of knives and guns, out of their boats. Though to admit the truth, they never did anything to warrant the white man's treatment of them.

Relations between the white settlers and the Indians had deteriorated steadily all down through the years and when in the more enlightened and civilized atmosphere of the early 19th century various governors attempted to remove this old suspicion and enmity, and win the Indians over to friendship, the task wasn't an easy one. So Governor Holloway reported to Lord Castlereagh, and proceeded to outline his plan of campaign. This was to have a number of paintings executed.

These paintings would show two groups of men—a group of Beothucks and a group of white men. Each group was to be shown dressed in their characteristic clothing. The Indians were to be shown bringing furs to the white men, and the white men bringing blankets, axes and so forth to the Indians—the whole idea, of course, to portray them trading on friendly and mutually profitable terms. These pictures were to be carried north to some part of the coast which the Indians were known to frequent, and left there. In this way the barrier of language was to be broken down, for of course the pictures would be so clear and unmistakable that the Indians couldn't help grasping their meaning and suggestion.

Governor Holloway estimated that a guide to lead the party to the best place to leave the pictures would cost about thirty pounds sterling, and he proposed further that an amount of fifty pounds in addition should be spent for the purchase of goods to be left there with the pictures. He asked permission to adopt his proposal, and Lord Castlereagh wrote back endorsing it fully and giving him authority to go ahead. Governor Holloway thereupon engaged Lieut. Sprott, a naval man attached to the Newfoundland station, to lead the expedition by schooner and to engage a suitable guide. Sprott took the pictures and the goods and, after taking the guide aboard, sailed down to Exploits Bay and went ashore.

To their regret there were no signs whatever that any of the Indians had come out from the interior that spring, but nevertheless he went a little distance inland and put the pictures in position at a place known usually to be frequented by the Indians when they did come out to the coast. The goods—blankets, axes, trinkets, and various other articles known to attract the Indians—were left beside the pictures.

According to the scheme outlined by Governor Holloway this procedure was to be followed for two years running—in the hope that after getting the goods left there the Indians would return next spring with furs and take a new supply of goods in return, the first lot in that case being a free gift to them. The scheme was to be tried for the second time, said Governor Holloway, "because these poor wretches have been so long ill-treated that it may perhaps take some time to wean their minds from the strong impression of mistrust which they have imbibed from suffering repeated cruelties."

Well, Lieut. Sprott returned to his schooner and waited around for a while— two or three weeks, probably—and then went back inland again to see if the Indians had made an appearance. Unfortunately they hadn't, so he gathered up the pictures and goods again and brought them all back to St. John's.

Next year, 1806 he went down again, but again there wasn't a sign of the Indians, and again he had to return with the pictures and goods. They figured that one of two things must account for the non-appearance of the Beothucks: either they had all died out and there were no more Beothucks in the country, or they weren't coming out to the coast any more.

The Governor leaned to the latter theory, because the Micmac Indians had been coming to Newfoundland from Cape Breton for some time past, and between these two tribes of Indians—the Beothucks and Micmacs—there was bad blood, very bad blood. The Micmacs were an aggressive and warlike tribe, whereas the Beothucks were anything but warlike. 'Twas the Beothucks who always came off second-best in encounters with the Micmacs, and so they had adopted the deliberate policy of avoiding their aggressive and quarrelsome enemies. That this latter theory best accounted for the non-appearance of the Beothucks on the coast two years running when the pictures were placed in position is proved by the evidence of Lieut. Buchan five or six years later, on the occasion of his tragic expedition into the interior in search of the Beothucks. He actually met and negotiated with the tribe-numbering upwards of a hundred Beothucks, while things he saw and heard led him to the firm belief that there were several thousand Beothuck Indians in Newfoundland at that time.

Well, it's too bad to realise that Governor Holloway's cleverly-conceived plan of bringing about friendship with the Beothucks collapsed as it did through the non-appearance of the Indians...all the more tragic inasmuch as success at that time might have, almost certainly would have, prevented the disastrous ending to Lieut. Buchan's expedition four or five years later, and might have established an understanding with the aborigines of Newfoundland for all time. It failed, however; friendship was never established between the white man and the Indians, and those pathetic Beothucks dwindled away in numbers until there wasn't even one of them living throughout the entire island. All in all, though, it seems that the name of Governor Holloway deserves to be remembered in Newfoundland history for this cleverly planned and ingenious attempt of his through painted pictures.

Vice Admiral John Holloway
Governor of Newfoundland
1807-10

* * *

The Last Duel In Newfoundland

June 1940

This is the story of the last duel ever fought in Newfoundland. It took place at Robinson's Hill, just outside the eastern end of St. John's, not far from Rennie's Bridge. It is believed that the exact spot is where Lt. Col. L.C. Outerbridge has his home built today, either on the present site of the house or not many yards from it.

The duel was fought in the early morning of March 30th, 1826 and one of the two parties was shot through the heart and died immediately. It all began over the card table, though actually the real origin was the love of two men for the one woman.

43

There was a military garrison established in St. John's at that time, and there was also a naval ship in the harbour. The two men who fought the duel were Captain Rudkin of the military garrison, and Ensign Philpott, the naval man.

The name of the girl in the case has not come down to us with enough historicity to be able to state it definitely. But she was said to be from one of the town's best families, and her name is omitted from history probably because of the scandal that ensued after the duel was fought.

Rudkin and Philpott were in love with this girl. She preferred Rudkin. And Philpott, being of a very disagreeable and ugly disposition, had it in for his successful rival. Rudkin, the garrison officer, was a gentleman, kind, good-natured with hosts of friends and very popular in the town.

How long the bad blood went on between them is not definitely known, but the crisis came when one night the two of them, along with some other officers, were having a game of three-card loo, a popular card game in those days. Philpott was drinking, and had a glass of whisky on the table beside him. He was in an ugly temper. The row flared up suddenly as Captain Rudkin won a hand in the game from Philpott. Philpott sprang to his fee and yelled that Rudkin was cheating—that he had taken a card from the bottom of the pack.

Captain Rudkin denied the accusation—denied it indignantly, and the other officers present backed him up. Philpott being fairly drunk by now, repeated and kept on repeating the accusation. Suddenly he flung the glass of whisky into the face of Captain Rudkin.

Rudkin kept his temper admirably. Instead of shooting Philpott there and then, he walked quietly out of the room. As he went through the door, he said quietly to Philpott: "You know what this means—I'll send my seconds to you. You get yours ready."

The seconds met. An attempt was made to get Philpott to apologize to Captain Rudkin, who was ready to accept an apology and call the thing off. Philpott refused, and duel was arranged for the following morning, March 30th.

Philpott's two seconds were a medical doctor and a brother officer from the navy ship in the harbour. Captain Rudkin's were two of his personal friends. The duel was to be fought with pistols. They were to stand back to back, and at the word given were to stride ten paces away from each other, then turn about and fire.

Philpott was the first to fire. He missed. Captain Rudkin, with Philpott at his mercy, fired in the air. One of the seconds, seeing that no one was hurt, exclaimed: "Thank God! now we can all go home."

Rudkin was willing to let it go at that. Philpott, however, wasn't satisfied. He wanted the duel to continue until one of them was killed. Philpott was a crack shot and this is probably why he insisted that they fight it out to a finish.

They began all over again, marched the ten paces, wheeled, and fired almost simultaneously. Philpott's shot missed, and in the dim light of the early dawn he was seen to spring in the air and collapse to the ground. He had been shot clean through the heart and had died instantly.

The news soon got about the town that a duel had been fought and Ensign Philpott killed. Feelings ran high against his killer, Captain Rudkin. He was arrested on the charge of murder and put on trial for his life. It was, perhaps, the most celebrated trial ever to occur in Newfoundland up to that time, and had Judge Bolton, who was very unpopular, presiding over the newly-constituted Supreme Court. It was one of the very first cases to be tried under that Court.

As the witnesses told their story, and the facts of the case began clearly to emerge—how Captain Rudkin had been so sorely provoked, but showed such admirable restraint, how he had fired into the air, how Philpott had insisted on a second shot, together with the gossip of the town about the love affair, and so on—the sympathy of the crowd in the court, and of all the town, except Judge Bolton himself, quickly veered around in Rudkin's favour. The jury retired and in about half an hour returned with the verdict. It was Guilty with a strong recommendation for mercy.

This verdict carried with it a penalty of imprisonment for life, Judge Bolton was furious. He ordered the jury to go back again and bring in a verdict of Guilty without any recommendation for mercy. The jury went back. They weren't out long this time. Their verdict was: Not Guilty. Judge Bolton, to his unutterable disgust, had to order the release of Rudkin. The spectators in court, and hundreds crowding the street outside went wild with joy. They seized Rudkin on their shoulders and paraded through the town singing and cheering.

From here on no mention is made of the girl and Captain Rudkin. It is said, in fact, that Captain Rudkin was heart-broken and soon afterwards left the country.

Today in the home of a prominent St. John's citizen there reposes the brace of pistols used in that memorable last duel fought in Newfoundland.

* * *

Mrs. Travers and the House of Assembly Furniture

December 1940

One of the most amusing incidents in the whole history of our country occurred in 1834. It had to do with the new House of Assembly, then in the second session of its existence.

The first general election under representative government had occurred in 1832, but it was not until 1833 that the first session was held.

Now the House was holding its second session, and right from the start of it the Assembly ran into trouble. It's all very humorous to look back on it now, but a great nuisance to legislators at the time it happened. For here's what happened: There was no Colonial Building in St. John's in those times—the fight for Representative Government had gone on for nearly fifteen years, and when it did arrive it took everybody by surprise, so to speak, to the extent that there was no suitable building ready in which to hold the sessions of the House of Assembly. Consequently that first session of the first House of Assembly had been held during the winter of 1833 in a private house—the house of Mrs. Mary Travers. That was made to do. It wasn't at all suitable or convenient or big enough, but for lack of a better place it had to do.

Now, in 1834, the House was holding its second session in the Court House—not the present Court House Building, but the one which preceded it, on the same site as the present one, or very close to it. But when the legislators filed into the Court House to hold their first sitting, lo and behold, there was no furniture! This was very puzzling to the members. After all, there had been a complete suite of furniture for the previous session, tables, desks, chairs, and so forth, all specially purchased for the purpose. This furniture had been installed in Mrs. Travers' house, and naturally the members expected now, when they went to the Court House, to find the furniture removed to there. But, no, not a scrap of furniture was there. They were in a fix—all dressed up and no place to go, so to speak.

They couldn't sit down on the floor. That would be neither comfortable nor befitting the dignity of men who had been elected by the people as their representatives and legislators. And even if they did condescend to sit on the floor, there still weren't any desks on which to do their writing.

Well, in the midst of all the puzzlement and excited talk amongst the members, in strode the Sergeant-at-Arms to break the news.

The news was this: That Mrs. Travers had refused to deliver up the furniture belonging to the House of Assembly. She had it all in her house, where the previous session had been held, and dared anyone to lay a finger on it!

As a matter of fact, Mrs. Travers had pulled a fast one. She had gone to the Court and obtained an order of attachment on every bit of it, and to take it away from her was to defy the order of the Court. And she had a good case, too. The House of Assembly hadn't paid her the rent for the use of her rooms when they had engaged them the year before. The rent was still owing.

What had happened was this: The House of Assembly in the 1833 session had clean forgot to pass the rent bill. The Government of the day had forgotten Mrs. Travers rent, and had neglected to submit the bill to the House for approval. Of course if it had been submitted, the House would have passed it, and that would

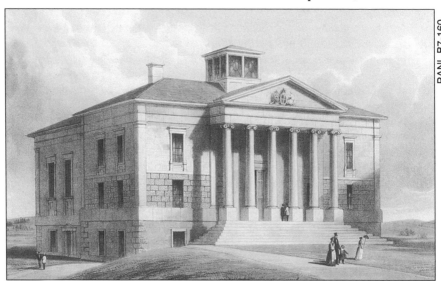

Sketch of the Colonial Building drawn by W.S. Best
(Opened January 28, 1850)

have constituted the Government's right and authority to pay Mrs. Travers. But as no bill had been submitted to the House, the government had no authority to pay it, and had to refuse to do it.

Mrs. Travers insisted on payment and the government explained to her that as soon as the next session of the House opened they would submit a bill right away for the House to pass, and then she would get her money without any further delay.

But either Mrs. Travers was sceptical of this, or somebody for fun or mischief got after her and persuaded her not to part with the furniture until the money for the rent was in her hands. Or possibly she was sore because instead of holding the second session in her house they were holding it in the Court House.

And thus we find the legislators meeting together on the opening day of the second session of the Assembly, and not a chair to sit on. It was a pretty embarrassing predicament for the government of a country.

No doubt some of the members wanted to have an order issued right away for Mrs. Travers' arrest. But while perhaps they felt like murder, the majority held out against any such drastic step, and a compromise was arrived at. This was to send to her right away, assuring her that if she would send along the furniture, the House would pass her rent bill immediately.

The word was carried to her. And she still refused. She was not allowing the furniture out of her house until the money was in her hands. At this the members got really sore, and a resolution was passed that Mrs. Travers be under severe penalty if she refused.

But even this did not scare her. She still refused to give up the furniture. And with this last refusal the House was stumped—they hardly knew what to do or where to turn. They could not very well buy a new suite of furniture. That would be inexcusable extravagance, especially as the amount owed Mrs. Travers was much less than the value of the furniture. And in any case they still had to pay her the rent.

The record doesn't say how they managed in the Court House during that second session. However, the whole affair was subsequently straightened out when the House appealed to the Governor to use his influence on the stubborn Mrs. Travers. The Governor sent word to her asking her to return the furniture, and assuring her at the same time that her bill would be paid without delay.

Mrs. Travers delivered up the furniture, and thus ended one of the most awkward episodes in a hundred years' history of the House of Assembly.

* * *

"The Banks of Nfld."

November 1939

One of the most popular of all Newfoundland musical compositions is the old song "The Banks of Newfoundland"—the air they've been playing at the Regatta every year for probably more than half a century. This famous air was written well over a hundred years ago, by Chief Justice, afterwards Sir Francis Forbes. Forbes was a Scotsman, born in Bermuda in 1774. In 1816 he was appointed Chief Justice of Newfoundland, and served here till 1823, when he was appointed to the Chief

Finish of a race, Quidi Vidi Lake, St. John's, Newfoundland

Justiceship of New South Wales, Australia. The air was composed by Forbes, therefore, sometime between 1816 and 1823, and is therefore at least one hundred and twenty-five years old.

* * *

Cabot Didn't Get Ten Pounds

January 1939

Margaret and all you other children who are listening tonight, don't you swallow that story you've often heard that John Cabot only received Ten Pounds English money for discovering Newfoundland.

Tens of thousands of boys and girls have been taught this tradition, but it's a tradition that ought to go, because there's no proof whatever that it's true, and is extremely unlikely in any case.

This story has always been based on the entry found in the diary of King Henry the Seventh. The entry goes like this: "1497. August 10th. To hymn that found the new isle, £10."

Ninety-nine chances out of a hundred this Ten Pounds was awarded, not to John Cabot, but to the sailor aboard Cabot's ship *Matthew*, who first actually sighted the land. This probability is given further strength by the fact that two or three months afterwards, on December 13th, John Cabot was granted a pension of £20 a year, payable half-yearly.

I don't in the least enjoy the role of smashing traditions—especially Newfoundland traditions—but it is no compliment to our country to say that its discoverer received the paltry sum of £10, and that it's highly improbable in any case.

Henry the Seventh, incidentally, was a very parsimonious monarch—loved money too much to part with it with any degree of cheerfulness, and it's an amusing sidelight on his character to note that even the £20 sterling he granted John Cabot as a pension didn't come out of his own pocket, but was charged by the King against the revenue of the city of Bristol, whose merchants had sponsored both of John Cabot's visits to Newfoundland.

* * *

Dempsey's Defiance of the French

August 1940

Mr. Bernard MacDonald of Englee, on the French Shore, contributes another most interesting historical sidelight on how a settler on that coast defied the French many years ago.

He was Jim Dempsey and he lived in Hillier's Harbour, a little cove situated midway between Englee and Conche. It was there he married and raised quite a large family who, as they grew up, moved off to other places along the shore, married and settled down.

During his sojourn at Hillier's Harbour Uncle Jim, as he was known, had countless scraps with the French authorities—those French naval men stationed on the coast for the protection of French fishing rights under the Treaty. One of these encounters ended almost fatally for one Frenchman.

Skipper Jim insisted on fishing with a codnet, something the French wouldn't allow. Just about as often as he set it the Frenchmen would remove it from the water again. But not being content with interfering with Uncle Jim in this way, they would also land in the cove and prowl around his premises after dark.

Now Dempsey, being an Irishman and living alone in such an isolated place with a family to protect, decided to put an end to this practice once and for all. He had repeatedly warned the French fishermen to leave him alone, but his warnings were ignored. So this time he loaded his big seven-eighth gun with buckshot and stood it in the kitchen ready to be seized at a moment's notice.

And not many nights afterward he was awakened by the French landing on his stagehead. He called out to them, received no reply, and let go with the gun, aiming low. He had the satisfaction of hearing a grunt and of seeing in the dim light one of the French marauders helping one of his companions down over the stagehead into their dory, and then row back to their schooner, which was anchored in the cove.

Next morning the captain of the French fishing vessel rowed ashore to Jim Dempsey's stage, told him that one of his men had been shot in the leg, and that as soon as the English warship arrived—she was due very shortly—he would report the case and charge him with attempted manslaughter or some such crime.

Well, the English warship duly arrived and Dempsey was taken aboard and tried and found guilty. The French expected that he would be put in irons and carried off to St. John's to enter jail. But instead for the next two months Skipper Jim had the time of his life cruising around aboard the warship living on the fat of the land and arriving back at Hillier's Harbour by her in the early fall. The warship provided him with a winter's provisions and a discarded uniform with brass

49

buttons which Dempsey always wore afterwards whenever he thought there was going to be trouble.

However, whether it was due to his uniform or his skill with his seven-eighth gun, he never did have any trouble with the French after that.

* * *

A Day to Remember

December 1939

The month of May, thirty eight years ago, was one of the most interesting and exciting months in the modern history of St. John's. It's pretty difficult, in these days of thousands of motor cars and airplanes, to imagine the tremendous excitement that was produced in St. John's on the first of May in the year 1900 by the inauguration of the street car system. By all reliable accounts it was a day and night such as this city has not very often witnessed.

Only one car operated that day, and it only ran part of the distance on Water Street—as far west, in fact, as Monroe's Cove. But it stirred up as much excitement, and brought together just as large a crowd, as all the airplanes we ever had put together. Water Street was jammed with people on both sides. Practically every man, woman and child in the city was on Water Street that day. They filled the sidewalk on both sides, they overflowed into the street, and they hemmed in the slowly-moving street car. They pushed and shoved and elbowed their way to get closer to the car—they climbed onto the steps, they climbed in through the windows, they filled the car to bursting.

For the whole afternoon the huge crowd remained on the street, travelling east and west with the car as she moved back and forth slowly through the thickly congested streets. Those who managed to get aboard the car sang and cheered at the top of their voices till they were hoarse—and jeered at those on the street who hadn't been able to get aboard. But when the car would reach the end of the run they'd all be pushed out, and there'd be a new headlong rush to get aboard, and the new crowd would take up the yelling and cheering as the car moved slowly back up the street, and so on all through the afternoon.

It had been rumoured through the great crowd that not only was the street car going to continue running back and forth Water Street after tea, as she was doing during the day—but she was going to be electrically lighted. Some people believed this—but the majority refused to believe. How was it possible, they asked, for electric lights to be operated in a car that was on the move.

There were excited arguments all through the day, and the tensest impatience existed for nightfall to arrive so they could actually see whether the car would be lighted up after dark and so be able to continue running just as in the daylight. Hundreds and hundreds of people didn't go home to tea—they just followed the street car back and forth along Water Street. And there were dire prophesies to be heard about the street car. To some people it just didn't seem natural or proper—it had the appearance of flying in the face of providence to be operating such a strange contraption. No good would come out of it—there'd be trouble of some sort, never

50

fear—and so forth and so forth. And surely enough there was trouble—trouble that very first day.

When the telephone system had started in St. John's some years before, there'd been almost, though of course not quite, the same excitement—after all, the telephone had followed long enough after the land-line telegraph and the submarine cable to be regarded as almost natural. And on the very first day the street car first ran in St. John's—that day on the first of May, 1900, the whole telephone system was put out of kilter by the street car. I don't know just exactly how it happened, or what caused it—but the central exchange was put completely out of commission by a flash of electric current that sent every keyboard fluttering and in a flash burnt up every bit of material of a combustible nature. From the central exchange it passed to a considerable number of telephones in private houses and caused the same destruction there. The damage done amounted to a very considerable sum.

But the funniest thing of all connected with the inauguration of the first street car system that day 38 years ago was the sight of hundreds of men leading horses, or riding bare back, around the town to get them accustomed to the new fangled contraption. Horses drawing long-carts, box carts, wagons, victoria cabs, slovens—horses carrying their drivers on their backs—big horses, small horses, all kinds of horses were to be seen that day and night—and there were dozens of upsets, dozens of horses reared and bucked and finally bolted like wild things up the first side street as the street car approached them.

All in all, when eleven o'clock came that night, and the street car stopped running for the night, and the crowd wended their way reluctantly back to their deserted homes, it was universally voted the most exciting, the most exhilarating day St. John's had seen for many a long year.

The inaugural run of the St. John's Street Railway, May 1, 1900

Newfoundland Power Archives

Trotsky Spent a Week in Newfoundland

June 1940

In the year 1917, up near Cape Race, the big Scandinavian steamship *Christianiford* was wrecked. She had 1100 souls aboard but not one was drowned.

There was one passenger on the *Christianiford* whose escape from drowning changed the entire course of the world's history since that year. If that man had been drowned in that wreck, there might be no Fascist State in Italy today....No Nazi State in Germany. No World War.

But he wasn't drowned, and in fact, he's living today.

The 1100 passengers and sailors were brought by special trains and steamers to St. John's, and accommodation was prepared for them in the Seamen's Institute and the Prince's Rink, until a big relief steamer could get here and take them all aboard. A few of the passengers went to hotels instead of to the Institute or Rink.

One of those passengers who went to a hotel was a man named Leon Bronstein. That was the name he entered in the registration book of the Cochrane House on Cochrane Street, and as a matter of fact it was his right name.

To the world Leon Bronstein is much better known as **Leon Trotsky** father with Nicholai Lenin, of the Bolshevik Revolution in Russia in 1917. Trotsky spent the best part of a week in Newfoundland. There is no record of his attempting to start a revolution. On the contrary, he kept very quiet. It was only a few months before that he had been put in an internment camp at Halifax, N.S.

When the Kerensky Menshevik Revolution broke out in Russia early in 1917, Lenin was in exile in Switzerland, and Trotsky was in New York. Lenin and his close associates got to Russia through Germany and Poland in a special sealed train provided by the German government. Trotsky boarded a steamship bound to Europe. The ship called at Halifax and he was taken off by the British and put in an internment camp. Trotsky invoked his technical American citizenship to be released, and when the *Christianiford* put into Halifax on her way to Scandinavia he jumped at the chance of getting to Russia, never thinking for a minute that he would be wrecked and be forced to spend nearly a week in Newfoundland.

There is little doubt that without his organizing genius the Red Army would never have been able to withstand the attacks of the White Armies. The Bolshevik Revolution would have been broken, and the whole history of the world since 1917 would be a vastly different story from what it actually has been.

It would be interesting to know if Trotsky ever thinks, down in Mexico those days, of the week he spent in Newfoundland.

* * *

The First Hospital in Newfoundland

September 1939

There are fifteen or sixteen hospitals in Newfoundland these days, but of course this wasn't always the case.

I wonder if you know where the first hospital was built?

It was on Military Road between Government House and Fort William, where the Newfoundland Hotel stands today, and was owned by the military authorities.

Afterwards the military people built a new hospital, on Forest Road, where the Newfoundland General Hospital stands now. And then in 1813, as a result of the agitation of the famous Newfoundland patriot, Dr. William Carson, a general hospital was built on the grounds now known as Victoria Park, Water St. West. Dr. Carson and Dr. Power were the two medical men in charge of it.

It was built largely out of funds raised by taxing all employees in the city a penny out of every pound received in wages, and by collecting a shilling from every sailor who entered the port. In the first year the General Hospital took in forty patients two of whom died.

In 1870, when the military garrison removed from St. John's, the military authorities handed their Forest Road hospital over to the Newfoundland Government, and the patients were moved from the General Hospital to it, the General Hospital being kept as a Fever Hospital, till in 1888 it was burned down by the fire department as a menace to public health. In the meanwhile, of course, the Military Hospital on Forest Road had been turned into a General Hospital and new wings were added from time to time.

Editor's Note. The first hospital in St. John's was built by the Royal Navy in 1725 on the southside of the harbour and served the ships of the Newfoundland squadron.

Military hospital off Forest Road, built in 1852.

53

INGENUITY

The Remarkable Propeller of the *Pelican*

August 1940

How many readers ever heard of the steamship Pelican? Well, that is one ship that deserves to be remembered in Newfoundland, because it was in connection with her that two Newfoundlanders once performed one of the most astonishing feats ever recorded in the long history of the sea anywhere throughout the world. The two Newfoundlanders were Mr. Ebenezer Bowering of Coley's Point, Bay Roberts, and Mr. John Shears Mercer, of Bay Roberts.

Before telling you of their very, very remarkable exploit here's something about the *Pelican* herself. She was a composite screw sloop—that is, a combined sail and steam vessel. She had a displacement of eleven hundred tons and carried engines of eight hundred horsepower. The *Pelican* was built in 1877 at the Naval dockyard in Devonport, for the British Navy. She served seven years in naval service on the Pacific station and eight years on the North American and West Indies stations, and also made expeditions to the White Sea and the Black Sea. In the year 1900 she was bought by the Hudson's Bay Company, and was used thereafter for twenty years in visiting the various posts in Hudson's Bay. 1920 was the last year they had her, and that was also the year in which this astonishing incident occurred.

She was down north as usual that year, and amongst her passengers were Messrs. Bowering and Mercer. They had been engaged by the company to build some posts in and around Hudson's Bay, and a lucky thing it proved for all concerned that these two Newfoundlanders, these two highly inventive and ingenious Newfoundlanders, were aboard.

On the fourth day of August the *Pelican* found herself in heavy pack ice in the Hudson's Strait. They made fast to a big pan of ice, but not long after they did several large icebergs began to drift rapidly toward them, so they had to slip their moorings and start the engines full speed ahead. As they were speeding away out of reach of the dangerous icebergs the ship struck a large pan of ice and two of her three propeller blades were stripped off close to the hub. A day or two later the third blade also was broken off, and her engines were thereby of course rendered entirely useless. Meanwhile, however, they ran up the sails and were able slowly to make their way into Lake Harbour, in Hudson's Strait, arriving there on the 6th of August.

It was at this point that the two Newfoundlanders, Messrs. Bowering and Mercer, having in the meantime got their heads together, approached the captain with a proposal that struck him dumb with astonishment and unbelief."Your engines are useless, Captain?" they suggested to him.

"Yes, with the propeller blades gone, they're absolutely useless," he admitted gloomily.

"You have no spare propeller?" they asked, and he admitted that he hadn't.

54

"But," said they, "if you had or could get propeller blades they could be attached to the hub and you could steam along alright?" they next suggested, and of course the Captain had to admit once more that they were perfectly right. "Alright," they said promptly, "we'll get you a set of propellers!"

"You'll get me a set of propellers." he repeated in surprise—"where are you going to get them down here in the far north? Why, there aren't any propellers within fifteen hundred miles!"

"We'll make you a set of propellers," they asserted with quiet confidence, and of course at this the captain didn't know whether to laugh or be angry.

"And how," he enquired, "how are you going to make propellers? Even if you had the stock, you haven't got the machines or anything else to make them. You're talking nonsense!"

"Oh, but yes," they retorted, "there's lots of stock around here—lots of big timber growing everywhere. We'll make you a set of wooden propeller blades!"

And that is exactly what these two Newfoundlanders did. Typical as they were of the proverbially adaptable and ingenious Newfoundlander, they first secured a couple of very big sticks—sort of hardwood—and having sawed them into the required lengths began with axes and adzes to cut and hew them to the proper size and shape. It is unknown just how long it took them to fashion out the three wooden blades, or how long it took them to get them attached to the hub and onto the propeller shaft. But it is known that having arrived at Lake Harbour on the 6th of August, she was able to steam out of there again on the 23rd of that same month, having been in there a matter of only sixteen or seventeen days altogether.

During that time, of course, the *Pelican* was brought in close to the shore and her stern tipped up out of the water to enable the fitting to be made. In fact there is a snapshot to show when she was so tipped up, and two other snapshots showing the two men working on the hewing and shaping of the remarkable wooden blades—the first and only wooden propeller blades ever used since steam began. From Lake Harbour she steamed about two hundred miles to Port Chimo, and from there she steamed back to Lake Harbour again. On the 17th of September she left Lake Harbour on her long 1500 hundred mile journey to St. John's, arriving here twelve days later, on the 28th of the month.

The wooden propellers worked perfectly. Of course, being wood, they weren't and couldn't be as strong as metal ones, and for that reason they couldn't put all speed on the engines, but had to keep the throttle down to lessen the pressure on the wooden blades. And to help ease the strain on the blades, of course they used their canvas whenever there was any bit of helping wind at all.

Mr. Miles, of the Hudson's Bay Company office was a passenger aboard her when she ran from Lake Harbour to Port Chimo, and not only that: he was in Lake Harbour when she limped in there in the first place, with her propeller blades gone. The *Pelican* was now considered by her owners to have fulfilled her days of usefulness, and for several years she was tied up to a wharf here in St. John's, until one year Mr. F. Banikhin bought her, loaded her with scrap metal and had her towed up to North Sydney.

Well, that's the story. You probably heard before of the time that the famous Captain Jackman rigged up a wooden funnel on his ship, when the original funnel was carried away by sea. You probably heard before of the time when the late Captain Barbour lifted the stern of the *Nascopie* up out of the water out at the icefields and had a new propeller put on in place of one smashed by the ice. But you'll admit that this instance of two Newfoundlanders actually making and attaching a wood propeller must be regarded as being at least as interesting and unusual as those other two remarkable incidents in Newfoundland's maritime history.

* * *

Made Boat From Bale Box

October 1940

Still another story illustrating the ingenuity and determination of the Newfoundlander—it comes from Mr. Albert Prince of Charleston, Bonavista Bay South. In the spring of 1932 he and two of his chums left their homes to go to St. Julien's on the French Shore for a season's fishing. They struck passage down with Captain Joseph Yetman on his schooner, and it was their hope, when they got to St. Julien's, to be able to rent the use of a fishing boat for the summer. They had no boat of their own. But to their disappointment there wasn't a boat there to rent—neither there nor nearby. Two days they spent looking for a boat, but there wasn't a sign of one anywhere.

Well, you can't fish without a boat, and it began to look as though their summer was completely lost. But they talked it over between them, and came to the decision that if there was no boat to beg, borrow or steal, there was only one thing left to do if their summer wasn't to be a dead loss; and that was to make one. And what do you think they did?

At St. Julien's there's a branch business of one of the big firms of St. John's, and to the premises of this branch the three of them went to see the agent. They asked him for a certain very big bale box or packing case he had there—he agreed to let them have it—and with only an axe and a hammer as tools they started to build a fishing boat out of its lumber.

They had it finished, and their first trawl set in the water, by the 25th of July. And by the 20th of September, when they gave up fishing for the season, they had sixty-seven quintals of fish to show for their efforts,—sixty-seven quintals of salt codfish, and two thousand pounds of green fish besides. Yes, and not only did they have this fish, but before leaving the French Shore around the end of September they succeeded in selling their boat for five dollars to John Davis and Sons. How's that for overcoming apparently insuperable difficulties.

POETRY

Poem on Newfoundland

In the Office of the Newfoundland Tourist Development Board in St. John's there is a large visitor's book in which some hundreds of tourists have written their brief impressions of our island during the past few years. Many of their comments are most interesting and enthusiastic. But one particular tourist wasn't satisfied to write his impressions in cold prose, but did it in poetical form, and here are the beautiful lines he wrote:

Would you see fair Nature's splendour,
Would ye wish to know the land
That displays the masterpieces
Of the Wonder Worker's hand?

Not the soulless gloss of beauty
That attracts the dreamer's eye;
Not the fertile plains of southlands;
Not the guileless azure sky.

But the rugged hills and gorges
Where the rushing rivers sweep,
And the mighty inland waters
Where the dusky mud-trout leap.

Or the wild expansive barren
In its pristine beauty found,
Where the twang of bow-strings hailed it
The Beothucks' hunting ground.

Come and see this sportsman's dreamland,
Feel the fighting salmon strain
Know the thrill of big-game hunting
In the caribou's domain.

If ye seek impressive grandeur,
Come and stand upon the shore,
Where the ocean vents its fury;
Where the mighty billows roar.

Listen to the eerie music
Of the seagull's screaming cry
Where the white-capped waves are hurling
Their defiance to the sky

Have ye seen the forest laden
With its argent robe of ice;
Watched the silver thaw transforming
Mother Earth to paradise?

Never artist could depict it,
Nor the poet's metric rhyme;
Never tongue could express the beauty
Of a vista so sublime.

Now I hear your eager question,
Where can such a land be found,
So beloved and blest by heaven
That all pleasures there abound?

Kindred spirit, friend of nature,
Let me answer your demand,
'Tis the Norway of the West World,
Tis the Isle of Newfoundland.

The Immortal Poet's Newfoundland Dog

July 1940

Lord Byron, the great English poet, was the proud and affectionate owner of a magnificent Newfoundland dog, which in all probability had been given him by his grandfather the Hon. John Byng, governor of Newfoundland around the middle of the 18th century.

And this same dog was the subject of what must surely be the loveliest tribute ever paid to an animal!

Byron's dog contracted hydrophobia, to his master's deep distress, and died, although Byron nursed him devotedly and did everything in his power to restore him to health. The great poet mourned the noble animal's death as that of a human being and buried him in the ruins of the ancient church at Newstead Abbey. Over the grave he placed a finely-carved pedestal, and on this pedestal he inscribed these beautiful lines of his own composition:

"Near this spot are deposited the remains
Of one who possessed beauty without vanity;
Strength without insolence;
Courage without ferocity;
And all the virtues of man without his vices."

The better to understand the respect and admiration implied by this epitaph to a Newfoundland dog, ask yourself how many men you've known who were worthy of such a tribute?

PANL/ A6-134

Newfoundland dog

These I Have Loved

December 1940

By Miss Maureen Murphy (With Apologies to Rupert Brooke)

The crackle of brown notchy twigs;
The chorus of a small gnat's droning whine;
The green-cloaked hills of spruce and dainty pine,
Basking in sunny showers of golden light;
A glowing camp fire on a summer's night;
Great mounds of mossy stones; and other things—
The long-beaked seagull with his soft grey wings
Skimming the foamy waves with startling scream;
And silver trout caressing the cool stream;
The sweet and sickening smell of pine-wood trees;
Ripe berries; gleaming oars; a soft sea breeze;
Brave fishing smacks a-trim with taut brown sail;
The haunting fog-horn's miserable wail;
Bright butterflies; and dancing whip-o-wills;
The cold blue mist that curls about the hills;
Old fishing smacks—all these are dear to me—
A fiery sunset mingling with the sea;
Pine cones; fir needles; a low wooden door;
And distant hillsides tinged with iron ore
Of red and purple tints; cold water shocks;
A cloud of spray, drenching the wet black rocks;
A cow-bell's tinkling music; winter cheer;
The gleaming yellow fish-flakes, tier on tier,
Nestling against the slopes of crusty red;
And Autumn's rustling sigh; the dim light shed
From shuttered windows; cool dripping eaves;
The sleepy rhythm of the tumbling waves;
Charred tree stumps; twinkling lights across the bay;
Pink salmon leaping in the sparkling spray;
The gentle cascade of a murmuring falls;
And ocean's tang; and bells; and timbered walls;
And wooden logs; and white and dusty roads—
All these have been my loves.

HUMOUR

A Newfoundlander's Quick Reply

August 1939

Mr. Arthur B. Walker, of Charlton Street, sends a story to illustrate the wit of the Newfoundlander—I'm afraid it's a bit rusty by now, but anyway here it is:

It happened in New York, where a group of men who happened to be of different nationalities were congregated one day, a Newfoundlander being one of them. They were boasting of their respective countries, and the topic turned to feats of fast workmanship, especially in the building line.

After they'd all had their say the American turned to the Newfoundlander and remarked:

"Nothing like that in your country, eh, Newfy?"

"Why, that's where we have you Americans beaten to a standstill," retorted the Newfoundlander, and then, as the American demanded to know what he meant, he explained: "On my way to work at quarter to seven one morning down in St. John's I saw a crowd of workmen excavating for the foundation of a big new apartment building, they were going to build. At quarter past six that same evening I was returning the same way from work, and saw the tenants of that new building being turned out for failing to pay back rent!"

* * *

The Right Rock For A Wreck

December 1939

This happened on the South West Coast in Fortune Bay, where an old fisherman owned a big boat in which he used to go fishing for quite some distance from his home port. This time he couldn't go himself, so he allowed his nephew to take charge of the boat and fishing crew. In a thick fog, near the shore, the nephew ran the boat up on a rock, almost high and dry.

A fisherman came out in his dory and remarked: "Well, you've run her aground."

"Yes, said the young fellow, "where am I?"

"You're on a rock," said the fisherman.

"What rock is it?" asked the nephew.

"The 'Conscious' rock," was the reply.

"Is there a telegraph office ashore?" asked the young man, and when he learned that there was he went ashore and sent a telegram to his uncle.

This is what he sent: "Crew all well—Boat on conscious."

The Wrong Time

October 1939

Here's one I'm sure you'll appreciate. It happened at the time that Sir John Middleton was Governor of Newfoundland, some eight or nine years ago. He was an enthusiastic golfer, and used to put in quite a bit of time out at Bally Haley having a game.

On this particular occasion his caddy was a young fellow named Jack Scurry—not the singer, but a relative. Jack Scurry was walking ahead of the Governor carrying his bag of golf clubs. The Governor was playing a four-ball match, and was accompanied by three well known businessmen of the city.

They were all trooping toward the eighteenth hole of the course with Scurry ahead of them. As he strode along toward the hole ahead of the party Scurry began to whistle shrilly. That wouldn't have mattered much, except for the fact that the air he whistled was the National Anthem, God Save the King.

Blithely he strode toward the hole, completely unaware of the havoc he'd created behind him. At his first recognition of the tune his caddy was whistling His Excellency stopped abruptly, stood stiffly at attention, with his hand at the salute. His three companions naturally had to do likewise, and there they stood, with game and everything else necessary cast aside, while young Scurry continued his whistling of the Anthem for a period of time that seemed for a while as though 'twould never end.

And did the young fellow blush when he discovered what he'd caused! His ears still burn at the thought.

* * *

Most Inconsiderate

November 1939

Here's one about the late James Stamp, a famous old time St. John's cabby.

He used to meet the trains to drive patients to the hospital, and did a lot of cab work for Government departments. One day he had to be at the station to meet a new housemaid who was coming by train to work at Government House. Mr. Stamp asked the conductor if he knew of a girl who was going to work for the Governor, and the conductor pointed her out at the end of the car. Mr. Stamp went up to her and asked if she had any valises or parcels. When she pointed them out he seized them and bade her follow him.

He noticed, as they left the car and walked down the platform toward the station building, that she was looking queerly at him. As they passed through the building toward the street, where the cab was, this queer look on her face became one of strong suspicion, and he wondered what the matter could be, so to make sure he said:

"You're the girl for the Governor aren't you?"

She said she was, so that it seemed o.k. But as he put her valises and parcels in the cab she spoke up: "I don't believe your're the Governor at all!"

"W.D.I.I.T.Y"

December 1939

Mr. W.C. Coffin of Joe Batt's Arm sends an interesting item. It tells of a young fellow in that place who went out on the squid jigging grounds in a brand new punt a few years ago. In a boat near him when he drew up on the grounds there was a fisherman who began to admire the new punt, and who noticed on the bow of the boat the letters "W.D.I.T.T.Y."

The letters made him curious, and supposing that they spelled the boat's name, and not being able to make out what word they spelled, he sang out and asked the boy what they stood for. The boy answered: "What Difference Is It To You." At this, of course, the fisherman got angry, and reprimanded the boy sharply for his sauce. But the joke was on the man all the time, because that was exactly the boat's name. It reminds us of a man who owned a dog, who whenever anybody would enquire what the dog's name was, the owner would reply: "Ask him." And that was his name. You can easily imagine the complications which continually arose.

* * *

"Let Those Now Bathe"

August 1938

Thousands of houses in St. John's have been connected up with water and sewerage in the past dozen years or so. But there was a time when there was only one bath in the city. That was back in the middle of the last century, nearly 100 years ago.

It was a public bath owned and operated by A.& R. Blackwood, and when anyone wanted a bath that's where they had to go. The papers of those days used to carry the Blackwood advertisement—"Let those now bathe who never bathed before, and those who bathed now bathe the more."

* * *

The Shortest Story Ever Told

July 1940

A man was walking along a country road in Trinity Bay, from one settlement to another. As he walked along he met another man, a trouter, coming toward him with his pole on his back and his trout basket slung over his back. Here is the conversation that passed between them. Said the traveller to the trouter:

"Arn?"

Replied the trouter:

"Narn!"

A Witty Newfoundlander

July 1938

I imagine that all Newfoundlanders who have been disgusted by the peculiar ideas so many people outside Newfoundland have about this country will get a kick out of a story that one of the soldiers in our Newfoundland Regiment told an English visitor at a camp in England during the Great War.

This visitor was quite curious, not only about the Regiment itself, but the country from which the Regiment came. "You have a lot of ice and snow out there, don't you?" he asked. The soldier's first instinct was to correct the impression by a simple denial—but as he thought swiftly, he figured there was a better way.

So he agreed, and said yes, there was a lot of ice in Newfoundland—and proceeded to tell him all about the ice. He said that the people built their homes of ice. Each family would begin building their house from the ground up, toward the sky, until the house would be 30 stories high. Then, said he, when the warm weather comes in summer the sun melts the house from the top story down. In some cases, he explained, the summer was over and the melting stopped by the time it got down around the ninth or tenth story from the ground—which meant that instead of having to build another 30 stories they had only to build about 20 or so on top of what was left standing.

By the time he got through, that visitor, at least, began to get the idea that his impression of Newfoundland's climate was a little bit astray.

$$* \quad * \quad *$$

He Got His Wish

November 1939

A certain man in St. John's bought a parrot from a foreign going sailor. That was when he was a young fellow. He was delighted with his purchase, and took the parrot home to his mother—but to his unutterable disappointment the parrot wouldn't and didn't speak a word. It was one of those most detestable of all creatures—a parrot that doesn't talk. So he swore that never again would he take a parrot that didn't talk.

Now here's the whole point of the story—when he grew older he did what many a man has been known to do—he got married. And the lady whom he married was one named Parrott! "And," he adds, telling the story, "I certainly got a talking Parrot that time—she's never stopped talking since!"

Several times he remarked to his wife that he was going to tell this to the Barrelman, and as she only smiled and said she didn't mind, he finally mustered up enough courage to do so, and that's how it happens that I'm able to pass it on.

It Was His Night-cap!

A correspondent tells me a story of a man named Dan Carroll. This is not the well known artist and landscape painter of St. John's, but a man Carroll of North River in Conception Bay. Mr. Carroll is a man up around 70 today, but he was always very active on construction jobs in Newfoundland and Canada.

One year he was coming back from Canada to Newfoundland via Port aux Basques. At Port aux Basques the customs officer asked him what he had in his valise. "Nothing but old clothes," said Dan. "Are you sure there's nothing but old clothes?" persisted the customs officer. "That's all," repeated Dan, "Nothing but old clothes—hardly worth looking at." The customs officer opened the valise. The first thing he saw was a bottle of rum. "I thought you said you'd nothing but old clothes," he exclaimed. "Sure, that's what I said." But what do y'call this?" "Oh, that—that's my night-cap."

* * *

Jack's Letter

April 1939

Mrs. J. McCarthy of Topsail tells a story about her father—or rather, repeats a story her father, the late Matthew Kent, used to tell. He had a man working with him. This man's name was Jack. One day Jack received a letter from his girl. He could read, but couldn't write, so after reading the letter he asked his employer to answer it for him.

When the letter was finished, Jack was asked, after it had been read out to him, if there was anything he wanted added. Jack considered a minute, and then said: "No, that's all—but you can tell her to please excuse the writing."

A RIDE IN A COFFIN

November's Ghost Story

November 1939

This story from Mrs. John McCarthy of Topsail happened in the Southern Shore settlement of Mobile.

It seems that a married couple living there a good many years ago were residing with the aged father of the wife, instead of keeping their own home. Apparently she was the only child, and so she and her husband decided to live with her father and look after him.

In a very bad spurt of weather one winter the old gentleman died, and then of course arose the problem of securing a coffin for him. The husband and wife decided to come to St. John's to buy one, and they tackled up a horse and catamaran and drove into town and bought it. The trip back over the road was terrible—deep snow, a high wind and quite a bad blizzard. The husband found it hard enough himself but what worried him most was how his wife was going to get on. It was altogether too bad for her to trudge along beside the catamaran as he was doing himself, and yet if she sat on the catamaran she'd freeze to death. He stopped the horse and put it up to her. They talked it over for a while, and then he made a suggestion—which was that she should get into the coffin.

" 'Twill keep the snow off you," he argued, "and you'll be able to keep warm." The wife finally realized the force of the argument, and got into the coffin. Of course he didn't screw the cover down, but just let it lodge on top to keep the snow from drifting in on top of her. Then he went up by the horse's head and began to trudge doggedly along through the deep snow. Meanwhile the wife inside the coffin—feeling weary no doubt by the drive into St. John's and the return trip—began to feel nice and warm, and as you'd expect she dosed off.

She might have been dozing for the best part of an hour when she was suddenly awakened by the sound of voices. One was that of her husband, the other that of a stranger. They were engaged in a hot argument, and as she listened she soon realized what it was all about. The second voice, as a matter of fact, belonged to a man from a settlement nearby. This man was coming from that settlement with a slide load of empty barrels, and as the road was narrow, neither of the two men wanted to run the risk of turning his horse aside to let the other pass, and in doing so probably get bogged in the deeper snow on the side of the road. Neither would move, and they'd reached quite an impasse at the point where the wife woke up inside the coffin. Wishing to be helpful the good woman pushed up the cover of the coffin a little and looked out at the road. She saw a place where the two horses could pass, and as soon as she did she pushed aside the cover altogether—sat up in the coffin, waved to the stranger, and said: "Here you are, here's where you can pass!"

The stranger looked at the woman in the coffin—it was just about dusk in the evening—and a look of petrified fright overspread his features.

Then he gathered his scattered wits together, gave his horse a terrific lash of the whip, and passed the slide and coffin like a flash of lightning—probably, if he's still alive, he's going yet.

Mrs. McCarthy, incidentally, had one of the most interesting hobbies, that of collecting the old dance tunes as well as airs of old songs and ballads of Newfoundland. She listens carefully to one whenever she hears it, commits the tune to memory, and than plays it on the piano. She has quite a repertoire of old folk-dance and folk-song tunes.

An early shot of Mobile

EPITAPHS

Newfoundland Epitaphs

March 1940

Miss Bessie Moss of Princeton, Bonavista Bay, sends several old tombstone epitaphs that she copies from time to time. The first one, she says, is inscribed on a tombstone on Long Island, not far from there. The man to whom the headstone was erected had buried four wives, and the epitaph reads as follows:

"An excellent husband was this Mr. Danner,
He lived in a thoroughly honourable manner,
He may have had troubles, but they burst like bubbles,
He's at peace now with Jane, Mary, Susan and Hannah."

* * *

Another epitaph is copied from an old headstone in Blackhead Bay:

March 1940

"In love I lived, in grief I died,
I asked for rum, but was denied."

And here's another one, at Long Beach:

"Here lies the man Richard and Mary his wife;
Whose surname was Pritchard, they lived without strife,
And the reason was plain: they abounded in riches,
They had no care or pain, and his
wife wore the breeches."

* * *

Another Epitaph

September 1938

And here's another epitaph. It's carved on the headstone of an old fellow who was a great lover of duck shooting in a northern outport. He composed it himself before he died, and it was carved in accordance with his own wish. It goes like this:

"Ye little ducks,
Lift up your head,
Your enemy is lying dead,
No more he'll point his great long gun
No more he'll make ye poor ducks run."

67

Another Epitaph

December 1938

You may remember that some time ago I read you a number of epitaphs found on old headstones in various parts of Newfoundland. Now a correspondent sends me another—but it seems almost too good to be true. I give it to you, however, exactly as it came to me. Here's how it goes:

"Here lies the body of John Power,
Who played with the gun at the Cabot Tower,
The gun went off and shook the nation,
And they found John Power at the Railway Station."

* * *

Newfoundland Epitaph

July 1938

Mr. H.S. King, of Catalina, writes in to ask me if I can tell him whether an old book in his possession has any value or not. This book has been handed down from generation to generation in his family for 264 years. The title page of the book was loose, so he enclosed it in his letter, and I notice that the book was printed at the "Sign of the Prince's Arm in St. Paul's Churchyard, 1673." I'm afraid I can't tell you, Mr. King, what value, if any, the book possesses, as it would be dependent largely upon the condition it's in. From the collectors standpoint 250 years is not necessarily a great age for a book. Mr. King tells me in his letter of a quaint epitaph on one of the old tombstones in the Anglican cemetery at Trinity. The epitaph runs like this:

"To young and old as you pass by, As you
are now so once was I
As I am now so you must be, Prepare yourselves to follow me."

* * *

Some years ago an old sailor man was looking around the cemetery, when his eye fell on this stone and its peculiar epitaph. Underneath the verse the sailor wrote these words:

"To follow you I'm not content,
Until I know which way you went."

68

Another Epitaph

This reminds me of another epitaph that can be seen on a tombstone in St. George's Bay on the West Coast:

"Here lies the body of Solomon Dawe, The finest man you ever saw.
Also his daughter Mary Ann, Who was killed by a fall from a catamaran."

* * *

Here's still another found on a tombstone at Belleoram, Fortune Bay, by the late I.C. Morris:

Man's strong desire for life we daily see,
And few who view this place would change with me;
Yet, serious reader tell which is best.
The toilsome journey or the travellers' rest?"

* * *

Another Epitaph

December 1938

Since I gave those quaint epitaphs from tombstones in Newfoundland cemeteries I've received another which goes like this:

"Here lies the body of Mary Jane,
Josiah was her husband's name,
She caught a cold in a shower of rain
And that was how she Heaven did gain,
She suffered much for a very long while,
And is not buried here, but in the
Straits of Belle Isle."

If you have any more epitaphs, send them along, will you.

MISCELLANY
Who Was The Veiled Lady?

June 1940

Here's another excellent story from Mr. Bernard McDonald, of Englee. Says Mr. McDonald:

"There's scarcely a cove or inlet from Cape Bauld to Partridge Point but has its little cluster of French graves, silent reminders of the day when France held sway over this portion of the Island. Forgotten for over half a century, these mounds of earth are unmarked save for the resting place of some captain or other person of note, whose graves are marked in most places by wooden crosses or perhaps in some cases a granite headstone. The latter, however, are few and far between, but at Fardy's Cove, on the south side of Canada Bay, there's a typical one that stands today as it did fifty years ago.

The vines and shrubbery have almost covered the little iron railing, but on the granite headstone itself there can still be read the inscription: 'EDOURD DUCHESNE, Marseilles, France.' Captain Duchesne can still be remembered by many of the older inhabitants as a kindly man who during his yearly visits to the coast always treated the settlers with the greatest respect and generosity, and his death (which occurred while on a voyage from France to Newfoundland over fifty years ago) was greatly mourned by everybody with whom he had ever come into touch. An illustrious kinsman of Captain Duchesne was Colonel Henri Duchesne. Colonel Duchesne commanded the guns before Verdun in the Great War.

In connection with Captain Duchesne's grave at Fardy's Cove there is a story that is tinged with pathos and romance.

About fifty years ago, not very long after the captain's burial, a large four masted schooner, presumably French, put into Canada Bay and landed a heavily veiled lady on the beach at Fardy's Cove. As though familiar with the locality, she made straight for Captain Duchesne's grave, and passing inside the little enclosure she fell on her face before the granite headstone. For more than an hour she remained thus, pouring out her grief, after which she departed silently to the waiting boat, and thence back to the schooner. Whatever the connection between the veiled lady and the dead captain was," Mr. McDonald concludes, "has up to now remained a deep mystery."

* * *

The Legend of Cape Broyle Head

September 1939

About thirty miles to the south of St. John's lies Cape Broyle Head, a very bold and picturesque headland rising to a height of three hundred feet above the sea. A very curious legend is attached to this headland.

Many years ago, in the time of our great, great grandfathers, a coasting captain noted for his savage, ungovernable temper was in the habit of visiting the Southern Shore. On one of his trips his vessel was becalmed off this headland, and was being dragged by the tide close to the shore.

The captain was desperate—his vessel was in imminent danger of being lost. He flew into a terrible rage and cursed his sailors, his ship, the sea and everything else he could think of.

"May the devil take vessel, cargo and all of us!" he roared.

And then, according to the legend just as she was about to strike, a great hand seized her and she was hauled bodily up the face of the cliff to the top.

To this day, according to the reader who sent this story, the prints of the devil's feet may be seen embedded in the solid rock.

The sender of the story has seen the Devil's Stairway, as it's called, and so have hundreds of others. Everybody confesses to being quite mystified by the presence of the strange foot prints in the rock—foot prints the shape of a cloven hoof, quite plainly shaped. Some of the oldest inhabitants of Cape Broyle have seen the timbers and wreckage of a vessel atop the headlands, though these have all disappeared long ago. But the imprints of the cloven hoof are still plainly visible, fourteen of them in a line, all about the same distance apart, all the same size.

And if it wasn't the devil that dragged the hundred ton vessel three hundred feet to the top of Cape Broyle Head, how did such a large vessel actually get there? Certainly no human hands ever dragged a hundred ton vessel up the almost perpendicular side of that high cliff.

PANL: A10-9 (Holloway)

Cape Broyle, 1890s.

How It Started

November 1938

I suppose that most of my listeners, especially in the outports, have often heard the old Newfoundland saying about "owning half the harbour."

This is one of the very oldest sayings in this country, but I doubt if many people know how it originated in the first place. The saying itself is used something like this: If a man in a settlement is inclined to be a bit proud or stuck-up, or people think he is, you're likely to hear somebody say: He's so stuck-up that you'd think he owned half the harbour.

Over 300 years ago John Guy, the first official colonizer of Newfoundland, who founded his colony at Cupids and also at Bristol's Hope, received from the King a Royal Charter granting him all the land between Cape Bonavista and Cape St. Mary's. John Guy wanted this territory settled, and one of his inducements to gentlemen adventurers from England was his offer to sell to either of them, for the sum of £100 sterling, one half of any harbour he desired.

A number took advantage of his offer, and thus arose, more than three centuries ago, a saying which you'll still hear in many parts of Newfoundland. Over in Brigus the Spracklin family are descended from one of those early adventurers who purchased from John Guy exactly half of Brigus Harbour, from Battery Brook to the Bridge.

The Pynns of Harbour Grace and Bristol's Hope are descendants of another of those early adventurers who purchased from Guy exactly half of Bristol's Hope, from Mosquito Point to the Pond.

* * *

The First Talkies

If I were to ask you when the first talking pictures were shown in St. John's, you would probably answer: "The Desert Song," at the Nickel Theatre, about five or six years ago. But you'd be quite wrong, for it's no less than 23 years ago that the first talkies came to this city.

They were shown in the Casino Theatre in the month of May, 1914, and consisted of the Edison Talking Pictures.

John J. McGraw, the famous baseball manager of those days, was shown in a picture on the screen, and you could hear him talking quite plainly as he gave a chat on the game of baseball. Then there was a picture showing a group of grand opera singers doing the famous sextet from the opera "Lucia." You could hear them singing as you watched the picture. There was also a picture of the vaudeville team of Seymour, Dempsey and Seymour, Kings of Mirth, as they cracked their gags and jokes. The talking pictures ran in the old Casino for a period of two or three weeks.

Billy Gale and the Prince of Wales

March 1940

Mrs. Patrick Dolan, of O'Regan's in the Codroy Valley has a very sound instinct for a good story—she always recognizes a good story when she hears it. And this one well maintains her standing as a story teller.

Mrs. Dolan tells of the time when Edward, Prince of Wales, afterwards King Edward the Seventh, visited Codroy Valley on a fishing trip. Before the railway was built, and in those days, perhaps even more than nowadays, tourists and travellers used to frequent the west coast on fishing and hunting expeditions.

One day, Mrs. Dolan goes on to relate, old Billy Gale was sitting in the shade of a tree near his house, pretending to sleep, but in reality watching a boat that had come along the river nearby. Some travellers were getting out of this boat, and his very pretty daughter happened to be working at the washtub near the door of the house.

He didn't know it, but one of the young men was the Prince of Wales. Neither he nor his daughter knew this, and they supposed that 'twas just another of those parties of travellers, sportsmen and tourists that were fairly common around there that summer. They paid no attention to the oncoming tourists, who were approaching the house.

The Prince of Wales led the others and he was a bit surprised that neither of the two spoke to him. Billy continued to pretend that he was asleep, while the girl went on washing clothes and didn't even look up. The Prince of Wales walked up to her and touched her on the shoulder to attract her notice. The moment he did there was a mighty roar. The Prince jumped with astonishment, and instinctively tightened his grasp on the girl's shoulder, as though to protect her. And there before him stood the old man, wickedly swinging his cane.

One of the Prince's companions, a titled gentleman who was accompanying him, hastened to tell Billy that the young man was the King's son.

"He may be the King, or he may be the Devil!" roared Bill Gale, "but he'll get my cane across his back if he don't take his hand off my daughter."

And the Prince had to do as he was told, too. But when Billy Gale realized that this was really the King's son, and the future King of England, he relented a bit, and during the three days that Edward remained there, during which a banquet was given to him at Chappel Green, Billy was one of his warmest admirers.

* * *

Is It A Tombstone?

October 1938

From the city a listener writes to draw my attention to an interesting sight he's often witnessed in around Topsail. If you travel about fifteen miles inland from Topsail he says, you'll come across a large river which somebody named Holystone River, because in the centre of the river there's a large stone and the stone is about eight feet high. It's perfectly square, just as square as though it had been cut by hand—in fact, this correspondent seems to think it must have been cut, because he says its face is brightly polished, and he wonders whether it was ever a tombstone placed there possibly before the river ran there—in other words, that the course of the river must have been diverted.

This large, square, polished rock in the middle of the river has me interested, because I remember that a good many years ago some archaeologists visited that neighbourhood, and declared that the fossil remains they found indicated that Manuels river is one of the oldest rivers in the whole world.

* * *

Advocated Selling Newfoundland to France

December 1939

If you were told that the famous newspaper, *The Times of London*—known as "The Thunderer"—had on one occasion actually advocated the sale of Newfoundland to France, you'd probably say "poppycock." But it's an absolute fact, and it's no thanks to *The Times* that we aren't a French colony today instead of a British one. It was on the 17th of December, 1890, that the famous editorial appeared. That was the time of the French Shore question. *The Times* started off by stating that some solution to the problem had to be found, and as France wouldn't consider selling her claims, *The Times* advocated that England should sell all Newfoundland to France as the easiest way to settle the matter once and for all time.

* * *

The Arch that Was Never Built

December 1939

What a pity it is that Mr. Stephen March didn't get his way in connection with the big celebrations that were planned and carried out here in St. John's at the time of the visit of the Duke of York, afterwards King Edward the Seventh, in the year 1860.

Mr. March suggested that amongst the various monuments, stands and arches that were to be erected there should be an arch across the Narrows. He was most earnest about it, too, and made strenuous efforts to get his plan carried out. *H.M.S. Styx* was in port at the time, and the officers of the warship accompanied Mr. March to the Narrows to survey and measure it to see if the scheme was practicable, and they decided that it was.

The archway, which was to stretch from one side to the other of the Narrows, leaving room for shipping to pass in and out, was to be gaily festooned with brightly-coloured flags, bunting and streamers for the daytime, and multi-coloured lanterns for the night. We have regretfully to report that the whole scheme was dropped at the last minute, for purposes of economy.

That particular visit of royalty to Newfoundland was the time the citizens' committee presented the Prince with a Newfoundland dog and a specially made cart. The sequel of that presentation is interesting—the citizens' committee bought the dog from a man who had one to sell, and after the presentation had been made,

The Battery and Narrows, St. John's, Newfoundland circa 1900.

and the Prince had departed, and the whole celebration had passed into the limbo of forgotten things, the owner of the dog was still struggling to get paid for the animal.

Saluting the Quarter Deck

June 1939

Last night a listener in King's Cove asked several questions. One at least of them was serious—"why does a naval sailor salute the quarter deck?" Tonight I've got a reply, and I have it by courtesy of Captain Schwerdt, R.N., private secretary to His Excellency the Governor.

Capt. Schwerdt, as an officer of the British Navy, was interested enough in the question to send in the required information, and here it is: the custom arose in the days before the Reformation, when all England was Catholic, and all the officers and men of the British Navy were of that faith. On the poop aft, on the quarter deck, there would always be a religious statue—and as the men approached the quarter deck they would remove their caps.

Long after the Reformation, after the statues were no longer there, the habit of removing the cap was continued, until eventually it developed into the present day salute. Now the salute is to the quarter deck in the connection being emblematic of the ship herself—and of course every sailor looks upon his ship, not as a mere aggregation of pieces of wood and metal, but as an actual entity, with a personality of her own.

Well, there's the information, King's Cove, thanks to Captain Schwerdt, whose kindness I'm sure we all appreciate.

* * *

A Great Broadcast

October 1940

With 250,000 people listening in the broadcast of Mrs. Ellen Carroll's 113th birthday at North River, Conception Bay, has been described as the greatest since broadcasting began in Newfoundland.

The broadcast which was arranged and sponsored by F.M. O'Leary, Ltd., was given from the Parish Hall at North River. The hall was crowded by Mrs. Carroll's neighbours and friends, and by visitors from many other settlements.

Sir John Puddester, Vice Chairman of the Commission of Government, was present on the platform. He read a telegram from their Majesties, the King and Queen, as follows:

Windsor Castle.
To Mrs. Ellen Carroll,
North River.

The King and Queen are much interested to hear that you are celebrating your one hundred and thirteenth birthday, and send you hearty congratulations and good wishes on this remarkable anniversary.

Sir John also read a message of congratulations from His Excellency the Governor and Lady Walwyn. He then, on behalf of the Newfoundland Government, presented Mrs. Carroll with 113 new one dollars bills—one for each year of her life.

The entire audience stood while their majesties' message was read by Sir John.

Following this, Mr. Frank M. O'Leary made a number of presentations to Mrs. Carroll. These consisted of his own and Mrs. O'Leary's gift, and gifts from a number of prominent St. John's firms, all of whom sent congratulatory messages. They were as follows:—Jas. Baird, Ltd., Riverside Woolen Mills, Steers, Ltd., Model Shop, C.P. Eagan, W.J. Clouston, Ltd., Chalker & Co., Ltd., M.J. O'Brien & Co., Ltd., Harvey Brehm, Ltd., A.M. Duffy, Ltd., Comrades of Sergt. Tom Carroll, Miss Margaret Kean, Dr. and Mrs. M.F. Hogan, Dr. and Mrs. Donel O'Regan.

Mr. O'Leary then presented a number of gifts from firms outside Newfoundland which he represented, all of whom also sent their congratulations to the wonderful old lady. They were as follows:—Pet Milk Co., Ten Test Wallboard Co., Blackjack Roofing Co., W.K. Buckley, Ltd., The Pepsodent Co., J. Lyons & Co. Ltd., Armour & Co.

Mrs. Carroll was greatly interested in the gifts, and as each one was laid before her she examined it closely, and caused sympathetic laughter when she picked up several of them to inspect them more closely. She was much concerned about how she was going to get them all down to her house from the hall. Mrs. Carroll said: "May God bless all that gave these presents!"

Following these presentation by Mr. O'Leary, the Barrelman read a large number of congratulatory telegrams from Newfoundland and many parts of the world. His Lordship the Bishop of Newfoundland, the President of the United Church Conference, Bishop O'Neil, and the Mayor of St. John's, were amongst the many who telegraphed. Captain Bob Bartlett cabled from New York.

The final event in the ceremonies was the appearance on the platform of the venerable Priest of Brigus, the Rt. Rev. Monsignor Murphy, who represented Bishop O'Neil, who was then across country on a visitation. Monsignor Murphy read the Pope's Benediction, which was conveyed in the following cable:

Cittadel Vaticano.
To Bishop O'Neil,
Harbour Grace,
Occasion 113th birthday of Ellen Carroll, the Holy Father imparts his
Apostolic Benediction. (Sgd.) Cardinal Maghone.
As the Blessing was imparted, the entire audience knelt.

Editor's Note: Mrs. Carroll died in 1942 at the age of 115.